THE
TAROT
ORACLE

Tarot Cards ✳ Runes ✳ Palmistry ✳ Numerology
I Ching ✳ Crystals ✳ Tea Leaves

Alice Ekrek

ARCTURUS

This edition published in 2012 by Arcturus Publishing Limited
26/27 Bickels Yard, 151–153 Bermondsey Street,
London SE1 3HA

ISBN: 978-1-84837-997-8
AD001893EN

Author: Alice Ekrek
Designer: Vivian Foster

Printed in Singapore

CONTENTS

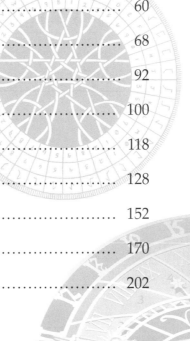

INTRODUCTION

ORTUNE TELLING IS A TERM WE USE to describe the act of predicting what will happen in the future. To find out our fate, we can consult an oracle, which is a person or an object that will help us gain a glimpse of coming events. Many different oracular practices have been used by humans through the ages to answer burning questions about what will come to pass. This book looks at some of those practices.

The use of these oracular tools and methods is often referred to as divination. Originating from the Latin divinatio, from divinare, meaning 'to predict', the word has come to mean reading signs and symbols which speak to our intuition, as if receiving messages from the divine. Often people who use these tools are seen as connecting with a divine source to gain insight and understanding of life – the present and past, as much as the future.

Divinatory practices that are popular today, such as the Tarot, astrology and the I Ching, help us make the right choices and bring the wisdom and the perspective we need to understand what is beneficial to us.

MESSAGES FROM THE GODS

The ancients had a closer connection with nature and natural cycles than we have today, and they looked to them for signs. Thus, many of the traditional forms of divination used animals, plants, stones, fire and water as tools for receiving messages from the gods. Almost anything can be, and has been, used for this purpose, and there is an idea implicit in the practice of fortune telling that the signs pointing the way are all around us. We just need to tune in to them and learn their subtle language to be able to use them in our own lives and gain the understanding they bring. The diviner learns how to read these messages and the meaning of the symbols that he or she encounters.

Today we continue to use many of the traditional symbols and meanings, although they have evolved and adapted with time. The way we understand oracles has largely been secularised – we do not tend to believe that the gods are the source of the information any more. Instead we have

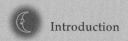

incorporated twentieth-century psychological language and theory into our understanding of the meaning of symbols in our lives. We now tend to think that the personal or collective unconscious underlies the creation of patterns of coincidence and connection in our lives and in the world around us. However, we also accept that the source of the signs and of messages we receive through them is a mystery which we are no closer to solving today than we ever were.

FATE AND FREE WILL

In Western culture these days we view time in a linear fashion, and the sum of our present and past actions (as well as external factors that impact on our lives) is thought to determine our future. Unlike many of our ancestors, we don't like to think that our lives are 'predestined'; we generally believe there is an element of choice involved. These attitudes affect the divination we practise today.

As those who use them will be aware, divinatory tools such as the Tarot and I Ching sometimes predict events that do not come to pass. One explanation for this is that our future is always shifting and changing, so predictions only apply at the time they are made. By this token, if we make deliberate changes, new possibilities may be set into action that can alter the course of our lives. In this way, with careful planning and persistence, we may achieve the outcome we are hoping for.

So consulting an oracle is not about finding out the inevitable, it is more to do with exploring things that will come to pass if we continue on our present path. The oracle usually has advice and insight for us in the form of symbols, which open our awareness and help us stay on the most beneficial path.

SCIENCE AND DIVINATION

So far no method of divination has stood up to scientific testing and verification and many people have asked why superstitious beliefs still exist in our current age, where scientific methods and rational thinking have the final word.

One of the counter arguments is, that while scientific methods and rational thinking have numerous uses and far-reaching benefits to humanity, even they have their limits. According to theoretical physics, for example, the nature of reality itself is unclear, and may even be shaped by the will of the observer. As the character Hamlet, in Shakespeare's play of that name, eloquently concludes:

> *There are more things in heaven and earth, Horatio,*
> *Than are dreamt of in your philosophy.*[1]

As 'rational' methods of understanding don't always give us the whole picture or provide us with the answers to the deeper questions of human experience, we sometimes look to methods that are part of our ancestral heritage and deeply rooted in our psychic memory. Indeed, often when people first explore methods of divination they report experiencing a sense that they are uncovering old knowledge they had temporarily forgotten.

As humans, we have a desire to understand ourselves and gain insight into our experiences. We have a natural capacity for finding symbol and metaphor in the literal world and gaining meaning from it and we often find that this brings the insight and understanding we crave. We also discover that learning these symbolic systems equips us with invaluable tools with which to navigate our path through life and gain wisdom in the process.

Although the results of prediction are uncertain, when we do get a strong sense of the signs around us and know something to be true despite the lack of factual evidence to support it, we can follow our instincts and try to achieve the result we want. In this way we learn to develop our intuitive understanding and begin our lifelong apprenticeship in the divinatory arts.

[1] William Shakespeare, *Hamlet*, Act 1, Scene 5, Lines 165–7.

THE TAROT

le Batèleur

la Papesse

l'Impératrice

Above: Tarot cards based on the
Marseilles pattern. Shown here
are the Magician (le Batèleur), the
High Priestess (la Papesse) and the
Empress (l'Impératrice).

Right: the Fool and the Queen of
Swords from the Visconti-Sforza
deck.

THE ORIGINS OF THE TAROT are not known, but evidence suggests that the cards as we recognise them have been in existence since the fifteenth century. The first set of Tarot cards we know of, the Visconti-Sforza pack, is Italian in origin; the second and more complete set is known as the Charles VI pack, named after the king of France at the time, although this deck may also have originated in Italy. The earliest evidence of playing cards in existence dates back to ninth-century China, so it may be that medieval Tarot cards were based on these earlier playing cards.

Tarot cards are thought to have been used in card games known as *tarocchi*. The only firm evidence we have that they were used to divine the future dates from the eighteenth century, although there is fragmentary evidence to show they may have been used for this purpose much earlier.

The symbolic images on the Tarot cards reflect the medieval and Renaissance European cultures from which they emerged. There were many multicultural influences in Renaissance Europe, including hermetic thought from ancient Egypt and Greece and other mantic systems such as astrology and the kabbalah. All these belief systems would have had followers at the time and the images on the Tarot reflect this. However, although the cards are clearly rooted in the ancient past, there is a timeless quality to the symbolism that speaks to people across cultures today and ensures their continued popularity.

THE CHOICE OF DECKS

Today there are hundreds of different Tarot designs to choose from, many of which have a theme or specific purpose, such as answering questions about love and romantic relationships or catering to every

interest, from pets to Arthurian legends. Given the wide range of choice, it can be difficult for the beginner to decide which type to select. Ideally we inherit our cards from a relative or friend, but many of us buy our own packs and let our instincts guide us.

One of the most popular sets of Tarot cards is the Rider-Waite pack. Created in 1909, it was designed by artist Pamela Colman Smith according to the instructions of Arthur Edward Waite – an academic, freemason and prominent member of the Hermetic Order of the Golden Dawn (a group

similar to a masonic order, but interested in magical and occult theory) – and produced by the Rider company. The Rider-Waite pack is now the standard deck and has been used as a template for numerous others. For this reason, we will look in detail at the meaning of the cards in this popular deck later in this section. Each card has its own meaning, which is applied to the context of the question being asked as well as to the card's particular position in a spread.

When learning the Tarot it is advisable to understand the meaning of the cards and then develop your own personal interpretation as you become more proficient. In this way, you develop your own intuitive system. You may also want to create your own deck of Tarot cards and personalise them by using the images you associate with the meaning of the cards.

The Minor and Major Arcana

The Tarot deck is comprised of 78 cards, 56 of which are divided into four suits and known as the Minor Arcana. The remaining 22 are picture cards known as the Major Arcana. Arcana is a Latin word meaning 'secret', 'mystery' or 'mysterious' and refers to the mysteries the Tarot helps us to uncover.

The Minor Arcana cards correspond with the suits in ordinary playing cards and with the four elements of fire, earth, air and water as well as representing other esoteric qualities (see Table of Correspondence on page 12).

The Major Arcana cards are not thought to correspond with playing cards. They are often numbered from 0-21, although the order varies slightly depending on the deck being used. They usually follow from the Fool card at 0 through to the World at 21.

The suits

In a standard Tarot deck, the Minor Arcana has four suits, each of which corresponds to a playing cards suit – the wands or batons (clubs), cups or chalices (hearts), swords (spades) and pentacles or coins (diamonds).

There are four sets of cards in each suit and they are numbered 1-10, with the ace as the first card. There are also court cards in each suit, although the Tarot has one extra court card – the Tarot knight.

Elements and qualities

The card suits also correspond to the four esoteric elements of earth, air, fire and water and their associated qualities (see Table of Correspondence on page 12).

TABLE OF CORRESPONDENCE OF THE MINOR ARCANA

Tarot suit	Playing card suit	Element	Season	Timing	Qualities
Wands	Clubs	Fire	Spring	Days	Action, creativity, energy, enterprise, intuition, hope, potential
Cups	Hearts	Water	Summer	Months	Love, relationships, happiness, harmony, sensitivity, emotion, fulfillment
Swords	Spades	Air	Autumn	Weeks	Ideas, communication, conflict, struggle, separation, resolution, change
Pentacle	Diamonds	Earth	Winter	Years	Money, work, talent, reputation, achieve-ment, stability, material realm

Timing with Tarot cards

If a particular suit is dominant in a spread it may indicate when an event is likely to happen. The wands correspond with springtime and action, so represent the fastest unit of time (days); the cups correspond with summer and represent weeks; the swords correspond with autumn and represent months; and the pentacles correspond with winter and represent a year.

CARE OF THE CARDS

Everyone handles their cards in their own way, but part of the ritual and etiquette of using a Tarot deck is to treat it with care. Practitioners are advised to keep the cards clean and wrapped in a cloth, pouch or placed in a box and stored in a private place when not in use.

It is advisable to become familiar with your cards and handle them regularly to build up a connection with them. In general, only the owner of the cards should handle them. In this way, you develop a deeper connection and when you come to consult the cards it is like approaching a personal confidante for advice. If you give a reading to another person (known as the querent), you may ask him or her to shuffle or cut the deck, but the querent's contact with the cards should be kept to a minimum.

PREPARING THE CARDS FOR A READING

Before the cards are laid out, they must be shuffled. It is worth focusing your mind on the question asked by the querent while you shuffle the cards. Then cut the deck once or three times and lay it out according to one of the spreads. Alternatively you can fan the deck out on a table and draw the number of cards required at random, placing each one in its position in the spread in the order you pick them. Some Tarot readers leave the cards face down and turn each one over as they come to them during the reading.

Card readings can also be given using only the Major Arcana. The reader needs to separate these cards from the rest of the pack and shuffle them as normal.

GENERAL INDICATIONS

When many cards of the same suit turn up in a spread, it could show that a particular element or quality is influencing the matter. If Major Arcana cards predominate, it may suggest there are wider forces at work and that external factors will determine the matter. When mostly Minor Arcana cards appear, it may suggest that the matter is in the querent's hands. Aces represent new beginnings and, depending on their position in a spread, may indicate that the answer to a question is 'Yes'. The court cards may represent people in our lives who have the qualities ascribed to the cards, or they may direct our attention to those qualities in ourselves.

TIPS WHEN READING THE CARDS

The Tarot is a complex system of divination. As with other forms of divination, on a superficial level it is just another form of fortune-telling. However, the cards have a deeper significance than mere prediction because they offer insights into the forces that are work in your life and within your innermost self.

We should remember to approach the reading with humility, compassion and sensitive consideration for all involved – including ourselves, the querent and anyone else who crops up in the question or during the course of the reading.

The symbols should also be treated with care and used to help both reader and querent gain insights that will be of benefit. Whatever the nature of the cards selected, the reading should never end on a negative note. If the outcome is undesirable, we need to take the advice of the cards and consider how we can work towards a better outcome. Sometimes the cards may indicate that our desire for certain things will not lead to the best outcome for ourselves. It may take repeated readings, with the same results, before we understand and accept this message.

Sometimes the Tarot can play up and will appear to give readings that don't seem relevant to the question posed. In these cases it is best to leave the cards for a while and start the reading afresh later on.

You have to work hard to get the most out of the Tarot, but remember that words are no substitute for experience and being guided by others is no substitute for using your own instincts. Surrender to them and you will be richly rewarded.

REVERSED CARDS

When cards are reversed in a spread, they can be interpreted as having the opposite meaning to the one they have when upright. However, some people only use the upright meanings of the cards. These are the meanings we will use here.

SELECTING A SIGNIFICATOR

A card can be selected to signify yourself, the querent and any other individual who may crop up in the reading. This card is called a significator, or signifier, and is usually the court card (page, knight, queen, king) which best describes the appearance and characteristics of the person in question.

The querent's astrological Sun sign may be taken into consideration when selecting the significator. For example, if the querent is female and her Sun is in an earth sign (Taurus, Virgo or Capricorn), then the Queen of Pentacles may be chosen to represent her – particularly if she also possesses the the characteristics of that card, such as generosity, practical talents and a strong connection with nature and the physical world. If not, then another card may suit her better and this can be chosen as her significator instead.

The significator can be taken out of the deck and placed in the centre of a spread, or next to the spread, to set the tone and provide a focus for the reading. Alternatively, the significator can be left in the deck; if the querent's significator then appears in the spread, it can be understood to represent him or her in the reading or the qualities he or she embodies.

TAROT SPREADS

A single card may be selected from the deck to answer a question, to provide general guidance on present events or serve as a focus for meditation. Alternatively, one of the spreads can be used to answer a question or give a general reading. There are many different ways to lay out the cards in preparation for a reading. Some of the more popular methods are listed here.

The three-card spread

One of the simplest layouts is the three-card spread (see page 16). The first card is selected and placed face up – this represents the past. The second card is taken and placed on the right of the first card – this represents the present. The third card is placed to the right of the others – this represents the future.

Sample reading using the three-card spread

The querent is a young female in her early twenties. She has raised a question pertaining to a relationship that has failed. She is asking the cards to shed light on the situation and bring guidance to help her move on from the heartbreak and give an idea of what the future might hold.

The querent has selected the following cards:

Card 1: the past

This is represented by the Lovers card, which describes the experience of a deep connection with another person in the past. One might surmise that this was an important relationship that has had a strong effect on both people's lives. They may have felt they had made the right match. It would not be surprising if such a connection was difficult and painful to lose.

Card 2: the present

The Sun in this position suggests that the most important focus for the querent at present is herself and her own healing. Perhaps the relationship has awakened her self-confidence and creativity. She should concentrate on her creative potential right now and find joy and satisfaction through achieving her own goals and potential. In this way she will gradually heal the wounds of heartbreak and regain a connection with the self that may have been lost or compromised in a relationship with another.

Card 3: the future

The Hierophant in this position indicates that the experience of the relationship has led to a growth in wisdom and maturity. A new perspective on the matter will be found. A lesson will be learnt and will result in the development of a new personal philosophy and outlook on life. It may lead the querent to take a course of study or learn a new skill which will bring greater personal fulfillment.

Since all three cards are from the Major Arcana, we can surmise that greater forces are at work and the matter is out of the querent's hands. Perhaps the failed relationship was inevitable in some way – the two individuals were destined to meet, but the results of meeting and being forced to separate will lead to necessary changes in the querent's life.

THE LOVERS

1

THE SUN

2

THE HIEROPHANT

3

The horseshoe spread

In this spread, seven cards are laid out in a horseshoe shape (see above). This spread is helpful if the querent has a particular question in mind or it can be used to give a general reading of current circumstances.

The meanings of each card position are as follows:

1 The past
2 The present
3 Hidden influences
4 Obstacles that must be overcome
5 Others' perspectives
6 The best path to take
7 The final outcome

1 Three of Pentacles
2 King of Swords
3 The Empress
4 Six of Pentacles
5 The Hermit
6 The Hierophant
7 The Ace of Pentacles

Sample reading using the horseshoe spread

A young man asked to have a general reading and selected the seven cards shown above.

1. The past

The Three of Pentacles in this position indicates that the querent has been working hard and learning a trade of some kind. He has proven his skills and abilities to others and been recognized for his achievements in some way. Perhaps he has been trying to work out which direction to take with his career.

2. The present

The King of Swords in this position suggests that the querent is in a strong position of authority at this time. Perhaps his mental and analytical skills are being put to good use in his work as well as his private life. Or he may be in a particularly rational state of mind, able to think his options through and weigh them up to make the right decisions. He may be called upon to help others do the same. Being a court card, the King of Swords may also represent someone in the querent's life who displays these qualities and has an influence over the querent.

3. Hidden influences

The Empress in this position implies that a feminine figure has a hidden influence over the querent's life at the moment. Such a card may represent his mother or another female in his life. She is working for his benefit behind the scenes, trying to steer him in the right direction without his knowledge and only wants the best for him. Fertility and pregnancy are also indicated – his girlfriend may be thinking about conceiving a child, so he should discuss this with her if he has not done so already!

4. Obstacles that must be overcome

The Six of Pentacles in this position may indicate that the querent's wish to share his wealth with others is holding him back in some way. Perhaps he needs to be careful with his resources and save for his future.

5. Others' perspectives

The Hermit in this position suggests that others may be thinking the querent is difficult to reach at the moment. He seems to have retreated from his normal activities and relationships to take time to think about his life and where he is going. He doesn't seem to have much time for his loved ones and they are no doubt looking forward to hearing from him!

6. The best path to take

The Hierophant in this position suggests that the querent needs to work out what is meaningful and important to him. Perhaps he will seek advice from a wise counsellor who can help to steer him on the right path. The querent has many questions about his meaning and purpose in life and may need to take some time to get in touch with his thoughts.

7. The final outcome

The Ace of Pentacles signifies that the final outcome will be the start of new business projects and ventures. Perhaps the card points to the setting up of a new business or to a job offer that is just what the querent was looking for. The purchase of a home, a sense of security and material comforts may also be indicated.

There are a number of pentacles in the spread, suggesting that career and financial matters are uppermost among the querent's concerns at the moment. Equally, the high number of Major Arcana cards suggests that there is a higher purpose at work; the querent can therefore trust that his path will unfold as it should.

The Celtic cross spread

The Celtic cross is one of the most widely used Tarot spreads today, covering general themes and providing a snapshot of a particular matter. In this spread, ten cards are laid out in the shape of a cross and a staff (see opposite).

The meanings of each card position are:
1. The querent (a significator card can be selected for the querent and used in this position or a card can be picked at random)
2. The obstacle or influences that have a bearing on the question
3. The question itself and the basis of the matter
4. The recent past – something that has just happened that has a direct influence on the question
5. The highest potential of the matter
6. The near future in relation to the question
7. Fears and concerns that the querent has about the matter
8. Other people's perspectives – how other people see the situation
9. The querent's hopes and wishes for the future outcome
10. The overall outcome of the matter

Sample reading using the Celtic cross spread

The querent is a man in his mid-thirties. He has asked whether he should buy a property, but is unsure if he should take on the responsibility of a mortgage at the moment.

1. The querent

A card was picked at random from the pack to represent the querent in the first position. The card selected was the Devil. This does not suggest that the querent is evil! It means that he has his own interests at heart and will put his needs first in this matter. It may indicate that finding shelter is a matter of urgency and the querent may find himself homeless unless the situation is resolved quickly.

2. The obstacle or influences that have a bearing on the question

The Two of Wands in this position suggests a lot of work and effort has gone into searching for the right home and that the querent has now stopped to take stock. Perhaps he finds himself unable to move forward to make the decision and close the deal.

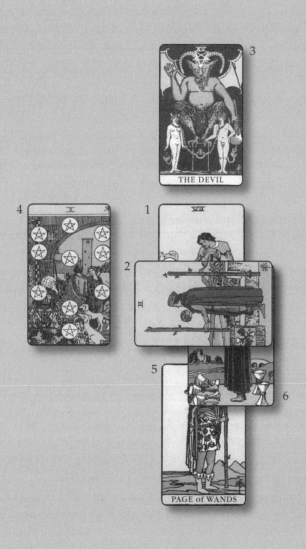

3. The question itself and the basis of the matter

The Seven of Pentacles in this position reinforces the suggestion that the querent is tired and weary after a period of hard work and research into buying a home. This may be deterring him from going ahead with buying a property. He is advised to stop for a rest and take stock of the matter before moving forward.

4. The recent past – an event that has a direct influence on the question

The Ten of Pentacles in this position suggests that material wealth and stability have been achieved. Perhaps the querent has saved enough money or received an inheritance that makes it possible to purchase a property. A great store of personal resources is indicated by this card.

5. The highest potential of the matter

The Page of Wands in the position of the highest potential represents a creative spirit who calls for excitement and adventure. This card may represent the querent's own creative potential or it could be someone else who has influence in the matter. This card suggests that the querent's priority is not to get tied down in one place but to maintain a carefree lifestyle. For this reason, it does not look likely that the client will be purchasing the property at the moment.

6. The near future in relation to the question

The Five of Cups in this position suggests that the client's dreams and wishes may be dashed. Perhaps the opportunity to buy the property he has set his heart on will be lost and disappointment will follow. Or perhaps a relationship problem or break-up will affect his decision.

7. Fears and concerns the querent has about the matter

The Six of Wands in this position suggests that the querent is afraid of success! Everything he wants is within his grasp but this may be causing such anxiety that he is unable to move forward. The querent should consider why he fears the possibility of achieving everything he set out to do. This card, together with the placement of the 5th card, suggests that perhaps he is frightened of the responsibilities that come with success.

8. Other people's perspectives – how other people see the situation

The World in this position suggests that other people think the world is the querent's oyster! They may believe he is in the enviable position of being able to do whatever he pleases and that limitless opportunities are open to him. Other people's opinions may be encouraging him to act cautiously to ensure he is not squandering the opportunities available to him.

9. The querent's hopes and wishes for the future outcome

The King of Wands in this position suggests that the querent has high aspirations. He dreams of travelling and seeing the world before settling down. The querent should follow his intuition and take the path that helps him to realize his dreams and achieve his greatest potential.

10. The overall outcome of the matter

The Six of Pentacles in this position indicates that after achieving his dreams the client will be able to share his wealth and success with others. While his wealth may diminish slightly (it was the Ten of Pentacles in the past, now it has been reduced to the Six of Pentacles), he will find a way to use his resources for the benefit of all.

The majority of cards in this reading are wands, followed by pentacles, which means that freedom and discovery take priority over settling down into a stable routine. After the heartache that may be on its way in the near future (indicated by the 6th card placement), the querent will be free to pursue his dreams and should follow his intuition in making decisions about the future.

The astrological spread

The astrological spread is based on the twelve houses of the Zodiac. It is laid out in the shape of a circular horoscope, with one card chosen to represent each of the twelve houses (see opposite page). If we compare the horoscope to a clock face, the first card is laid at nine o'clock, the second at eight o'clock and so on, in an anti-clockwise direction, with the twelfth card at ten o'clock. This spread is often used to get a snapshot of the querent's life at the moment and can answer questions about various aspects, such as relationships and career.

1   Eight of Pentacles
2   Nine of Cups
3   Ace of Cups
4   Eight of Cups
5   Seven of Cups
6   The Emperor
7   Knight of Wands
8   Page of Pentacles
9   Five of Wands
10 Ace of Pentacles
11 Strength
12 Ace of Wands

The areas of life covered by each card position are as follows:
1   The querent's appearance and persona
2   Personal values and monetary matters
3   Communications and short journeys
4   Home and family
5   Romance, creativity and children
6   Work and health
7   Relationships and business partnerships
8   Shared resources, inheritance and secrets
9   Teaching, learning and long journeys
10 Vocation, career goals and aspirations
11 Friends, groups and community
12 Unconscious and hidden realm

Sample reading using the astrological spread

The querent is a female in her early forties who would like a general reading about relationships and career matters. We can look to the 5th and 7th house positions in particular to describe relationships, and the 2nd, 6th and 10th houses for an indication of career prospects, although all the cards have a bearing on the chart. We should also look at each house position to get a general picture of a person's current experiences.

The querent has selected the following cards:

1. The querent's appearance and persona
The Eight of Pentacles in this position suggests that the querent is working hard to achieve her goals and perhaps training and learning new skills. To others, she might seem consumed by work at the moment and very serious about her career.

2. Personal values and monetary matters
The Nine of Cups in this position indicates that great wealth and emotional security are possible. Work is extremely satisfying and rewarding. If this does not describe

the querent's current job, it should do so in the near future if the querent continues on her current path.

3. Communications and short journeys
The Ace of Cups in this position describes the ability to communicate with others from the heart. A new friendship or romance may begin as the result of a chance meeting while on a short journey. A love letter may be on its way.

4. Home and family
The Eight of Cups in this position suggests that the querent needs some time away from her home and family to gain some perspective and learn to appreciate them again. It also indicates that it might be helpful for the querent to explore her family background and roots.

5. Romance, creativity and children
The Seven of Cups in this position points to the need to make a decision regarding a lover. If it is relevant, there may be a choice involving children. The querent may be feeling creative at this time and should listen to messages arising out of the imagination and dreams to help her come to a decision.

6. Work and health
The Emperor in this position suggests that a decision needs to be made about the querent's job. This could involve taking on increased responsibilities as well as the wider decision about what job the querent really wants to be doing. The Emperor card recommends self-discipline and suggests that a father figure may have influence over the querent's decisions. The querent should make sure she fulfills her responsibilities at work and maintains a good healthcare regime.

7. Relationships and business partnerships
The Knight of Wands in this position represents a current partner or person about to enter the querent's life, who is fiery, courageous and brash. Perhaps the querent has had an argument with her partner that has resulted in angry scenes and caused her to question the relationship. The card might also signify that the querent's love life is about to take a new direction.

8. Shared resources, inheritance and secrets
The Page of Pentacles in this position indicates that the querent is being sensible with money and in matters that have been entrusted to her. She may

be relied upon to keep a secret. In this placement, the card also suggests the querent has inherited a sense of responsibility and strong work ethic from her parents.

9. Teaching, learning and long journeys

The Five of Wands in this position suggests a crisis in the querent's personal philosophies and beliefs. Perhaps the fiery arguments with her partner stem from this. The querent may need to visit a conflict zone or she may be met with hostility when travelling to a distant location. As indicated by the 1st card in the spread, she is currently working to develop a new skill but may encounter obstacles that impact on her learning. The problem needs to be addressed head on and a resolution found.

10. Vocation, career goals and aspirations

The Ace of Pentacles in this position represents great material rewards and achievements in the querent's career and chosen profession. Perhaps a new job opportunity or business venture is imminent. This placement indicates that the querent is on the right track to achieve her career goals and ambitions. Her hard work and diligence will pay off.

11. Friends, groups and community

The Strength card in this position shows that the querent is regarded highly by her friends and wider community. While she encounters conflict in other parts of her life, the querent is in a strong position to work for the benefit of those around her and may be asked to defend friends who are in need of assistance.

12. Unconscious and hidden realm

The Ace of Wands in this position is an interesting placement for such a lively and active card. It could suggest that the querent's intuition is particularly strong at this time and she should use it to navigate the way ahead. She may also need to explore her anger, which may be rumbling beneath the surface and could be a reason for the conflicts encountered in her relationships.

Overall, there are mostly cups and pentacles in this reading, reflecting the focus of the question which was on relationships (cups) and career matters (pentacles). It looks as though important decisions need to be made in both areas and that the querent has the diligence and commitment to succeed along whichever path she chooses.

THE MEANING OF THE CARDS – THE MAJOR ARCANA

The 22 cards of the Major Arcana represent archetypal qualities of the human psyche and the different stages of personal experience familiar to us all. Starting with the Fool, they describe our journey through life, ending with the World and then returning full circle back to the Fool again. In this way, the journey is continued and taken to the next level according to the cycle of life.

0 The Fool

Keywords: fresh start, beginning, freedom, courage, openness, trust, risk-taking

The Fool is shown standing on the edge of a precipice, bag and rose in hand, with a dog at his heels. He is stepping into the unknown, alone except for his trusty dog, full of expectation and potential and unfettered by the doubts and cynicism that come with experience. The card suggests a choice must be made and a journey started into unknown territory. Courage is required to take the first step. The Fool is unaware of and unprepared for what awaits him, but through new experiences will discover his true potential.

1 The Magician

Keywords: skills, potential, mastery, resourcefulness, will, power, creativity, action

The Magician stands next to a table upon which lie a wand, a sword, a chalice and a pentacle. These represent the four Tarot suits and the four elements. Wand in hand, the Magician is about use his powers to command his will. Above his head the infinity symbol, known as the cosmic lemniscate, represents the eternal and immortal force of energy. At this first stage of his journey, the Fool realizes that he has all the resources he needs to gain mastery over the material world of opposites and duality. The Magician is an authority figure who has the power to do good. Creativity and resourcefulness are needed to overcome obstacles.

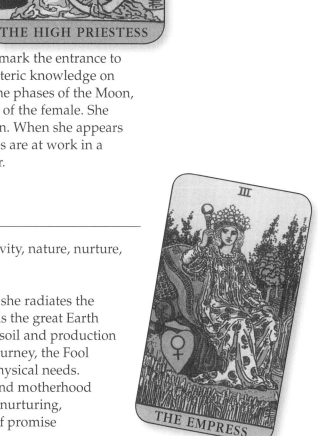

THE HIGH PRIESTESS

2 The High Priestess

Keywords: wisdom, intuition, mystery, secrets, hidden knowledge, unseen influences at work

The High Priestess is also described as the veiled Isis. She is seated between two pillars which represent the great universal principles and mark the entrance to the sacred temple. She holds a scroll containing esoteric knowledge on her lap. On her forehead she wears the symbol of the phases of the Moon, representing the cycles of life and the creative force of the female. She stands for hidden knowledge, wisdom and intuition. When she appears in a spread it could indicate that some hidden forces are at work in a situation and one must look inwards for the answer.

3 The Empress

Keywords: abundance, pleasure, contentment, creativity, nature, nurture, balance, fullness, fertility, renewal

The Empress is Isis unveiled. Seated on her throne, she radiates the beauty that comes from harmony with nature. She is the great Earth Mother, in charge of the seasons, the fertility of the soil and production of the food which sustains us. At this stage of the journey, the Fool realizes that he needs to look after his health and physical needs. The Empress indicates the possibility of marriage and motherhood as well as material gain. With careful attention and nurturing, a creative project will bear fruit. A situation is full of promise and has great potential.

THE EMPRESS

4 The Emperor

Keywords: judgement, decision, action, responsibility, challenge, effectiveness, satisfaction from achievement

The Emperor is the card of fathering and indicates focus and the energy of accomplishment. The Emperor challenges the Fool to build something lasting to be proud of. The Fool is asked to make a decision about what he wants and what he values most in the world. He must then set out to achieve his goal. It will require hard work and unwavering determination and he will be judged on his abilities and the way in which he exercises responsibility. When this card is drawn, someone in a position of authority may offer advice that should be taken seriously.

5 The Hierophant

Keywords: law, tradition, religion, meaning, philosophy, teaching, learning, vision

Also called the High Priest or Pope, the Hierophant is a wise teacher, priest or counsellor to whom we may turn at times of personal crisis. Like the High Priestess, the Hierophant is seated between two pillars at the entrance of the temple. However, unlike the High Priestess, the Hierophant represents the outer trappings and traditions of religious practice. At this stage in his journey the Fool must find meaning and seek answers to questions about the purpose of his life. When this card appears in a spread it indicates that we may be searching for meaning and need to approach a situation with a philosophical outlook.

6 The Lovers

Keywords: love, connection, sexual attraction, union of opposites, new possibilities, temptation, choice

In the card of the Lovers, we find a naked man and woman standing next to (and, in some versions, embracing) each other, with the man looking at the woman. The woman is looking up to the sky, where Cupid is watching. The card alludes to the first lovers of the Old Testament – Adam and Eve in the Garden of Eden. Thus, along with love, relationship and the family, the card of the Lovers has come to represent temptation and the need to make a choice. At this stage of his journey, the Fool finds his match and decides to marry and unite the opposites within. The card suggests that a union is possible and there is hope for a bright future ahead.

7 The Chariot

Keywords: action, control, focus, strength, stability, willpower, conflict, struggle, change, triumph

The Chariot card represents gaining control over conflicting forces. The charioteer in the card is trying to control the two sphinxes which are pulling the chariot. The sphinxes – one black, one white – represent principles pulling in opposite directions. The opposites that were united in the previous Lovers card must now be kept moving in the same direction. At this stage in his journey, the Fool must use all his strength to keep on the right track. By seeing what has to be done and taking control of the situation, obstacles will be overcome. If we manage to keep the opposite forces on the same path, we will go far. Events are moving quickly.

8 Strength

Keywords: strength, control, confidence, balance, integrity, courage, generosity, compassion

The card of Strength depicts a woman holding open (or forcing closed) the jaws of a lion, apparently without fear of danger. The lion represents our primal urges, the wild and ravenous beast within, yet the woman has succeeded in taming them. Like the Magician, she has an infinity symbol, or cosmic leminiscate, above her head, indicating that she has achieved a new level of consiousness and understanding. The Fool is gaining mastery over the primal forces that have governed him and his conscious ego is taking control. The card suggests that struggles may be ahead, but we have the courage and confidence to overcome any danger.

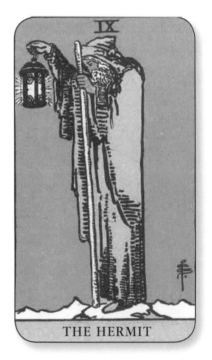

9 The Hermit

Keywords: solitude, withdrawal, detachment, caution, patience, prudence, discretion, limitation

The Hermit stands alone on a mountaintop, holding up a lamp to light his way. He is wearing a cloak and carrying a staff to help him through the tough terrain. He has retreated from society to gain some perspective and look inward for answers. Through patient searching, he gains insight and connects with his intuitive knowledge. The Fool has reached maturity and questions his direction in life. When the Hermit appears in a spread, we may need to retreat from a situation so that we can recharge our batteries and have space to think. We are advised to retreat and work out what is important to us before taking any further action in a matter.

10 Wheel of Fortune

Keywords: luck, chance, fortune, destiny, change, success, new direction

The Wheel of Fortune represents an unexpected element that will change the outcome of a matter. It may be good or bad, but generally indicates a turn of luck for the better and may herald opportunities and a new phase in life. Although we are responsible for shaping our own lives, this card suggests that luck and fortune may come along at any moment and change things for the better. When the Wheel of Fortune is drawn, an unexpected solution to a problem may present itself. Sometimes the card reminds us that 'what goes around comes around', and that past actions will be rewarded.

11 Justice

Keywords: fairness, impartiality, balance, reflection, decision, equality, truth

Like the High Priestess and Hierophant, justice is seated between two pillars, suggesting a religious connection. Justice is one of the universal principles upon which society is built. The figure in the card holds a sword and points it upwards, indicating that justice will be upheld. The sword of justice is famously double-edged, however and a balance must be found between two opposing sides for there to be a fair outcome. Following the Wheel of Fortune card, Justice reminds us that we are accountable for our actions and urges us to be honest and fair. This card indicates that justice will prevail.

12 The Hanged Man

Keywords: patience, waiting, surrender, sacrifice, wisdom, foresight, planning, strategy, eventual gain

The card of the Hanged Man depicts a man hanging upside down from a beam. His legs are crossed and he has reached an impasse. No further movement is possible for the time being. The card represents sacrifice and the willingness to face short-term losses to ensure long-term gains. The Fool must learn patience and how to act strategically to achieve the result he wants. An immediate advantage must be given up, but will eventually be replaced by a much better opportunity. All expectations should be surrendered for the time being.

13 Death

Keywords: endings, loss, mourning, acceptance, adjustment, change, transition, rebirth, renewal

The card of Death is represented by a skeleton in armour riding a white horse over the corpse of a king. This suggests that the old order has ended and a new era is about to begin. At this stage in the journey, the Fool must accept approaching endings and uncertainty about the future. The endings may be difficult and painful, but we must learn to accept them. After a period of mourning and adjustment, we will be able to move on and embark on a new path. Change is inevitable. As we come to terms with loss, we are transformed.

14 Temperance

Keywords: balanced temperament, harmony, moderation, cooperation, compromise, adaptability, relationship

The Temperance card shows the figure of an angel pouring liquid from one vessel into another. This indicates that feelings are able to flow freely. It may signify a guardian angel watching over us. The card represents balance, healing and harmony. The Fool has learnt to master his thoughts and feelings and can now have harmonious relationships with others. We should act in moderation; compromise is the key to any problem. We have the ability to manage a situation and resolve problems. Events will run smoothly and success can be achieved. This card indicates that good relationships are possible.

15 The Devil

Keywords: lust, greed, rage, primal instincts, secrets, the shadow, success in career and personal interests

The Devil card may fill us with fear and dread because the Devil is a Christian symbol associated with evil. The card does not indicate evil, but asks us to confront the shadowy, instinctual part of ourselves. Following the perfect balance of the angel in the Temperance card, the Fool is reminded of those parts of himself that are self-serving and uncooperative, which he had tried to keep hidden away even from himself. When this card appears in a spread, things that we don't like to admit about our own character and desires may be trying to break into our consciousness. We may encounter these unwelcome qualities in others or in our dreams. A neglected part of us needs to be heard. Personal gain and success in our career is indicated by this card. We are advised to act in our own interests.

16 The Tower

Keywords: conflict, overthrow, disruption, disapproval, unexpected change

The Tower card shows a tall building that has been struck by lightning. It is in flames and about to topple over. The lightning signifies that the gods are angry or disapproving. The Fool encounters sudden and disruptive changes and crises which force him to question his journey. This card suggests that the times are volatile, things are not going according to plan and the old order is in danger of being overthrown. We should not try to hold on and save the toppling tower; it is better to stand back and wait for things to settle. We may face uncertainty for a while. This card asks us to re-evaluate our current path. A sudden, complete change may be the best way forward.

17 The Star

Keywords: hope, faith, meaning, inspiration, promise, healing, protection, new horizon

The Star is a welcome symbol of hope, inspiration and rebirth to the Fool in the wake of the difficulties and uncertainties encountered in the Devil and Tower cards. In this card we see a star shining brightly in the sky above a beautiful woman who is emptying jugs of water into a stream. It represents feelings being returned to their source. Healing is possible and our sense of wellbeing is renewed. There is hope for the future and new possibilities are beginning to form. We are ready to give and receive love. The Star promises change for the better. This is a good time to meet new people, apply for jobs and aspire towards what is really important to us.

18 The Moon

Keywords: intuition, imagination, dreams, unconscious, fears, confusion, deception, disillusionment

The Moon is associated with night, the unconscious realm and the dream world, where our deepest fears and imaginations run wild. The Fool has encountered a period of confusion and disillusionment. Where is the promise of the previous card and what does the journey hold next? Situations are vague and unclear; matters are not what they seem. We can act without being seen! We are advised to avoid deception and paranoia. At this time we can more easily tap into our unconscious and find creative solutions to problems. The way ahead is foggy, but we should allow our intuition to guide us.

19 The Sun

Keywords: joy, optimism, clarity, trust, courage, ambition, success, opportunity, health, vitality, happiness

The Sun, shown shining on a child riding a white horse, is symbolic of life in full bloom. The Fool has passed through his dark night and the way ahead is clear again. He knows where he is going and what he wants to achieve and he meets with success in all his endeavours. Indicating energy, joy, optimism and worldly success, this card suggests that it is the perfect moment to embrace opportunities and live life to the full. When this card appears in a spread, it promises health, happiness and perhaps the birth of a baby.

20 Judgement

Keywords: reward for past effort, re-evaluation, responsibility, outcome, resolution, acceptance

The Judgement card shows an angel, possibly Gabriel, sounding a trumpet above figures rising from their graves. It echoes the Day of Judgement referred to in the Bible, when Christ and his angels will return to Earth and even the dead will be judged on their deeds. This card can be understood to bring us the reward in life that we deserve. The Fool is forced to look at where he has come from, how he has behaved and the choices he has made. It marks a point at which we must re-evaluate our lives. We may need to learn hard lessons and be held responsible for past actions. We are advised to come to a resolution and move on with a clean slate. The card can also refer to judgements in law.

21 The World

Keywords: integration, fulfillment, achievement, completion, ending, final reward, success

The World, represented by a dancing woman, is the final card in one complete cycle. The creatures at each corner of this card signify the four elements – fire (lion), earth (bull), air (eagle) and water (merman) – that form the fabric of our world. The Fool has accomplished much and learnt what he is capable of along the way. Challenges have been faced and battles fought and won. He is now ready to resume his position at the start of a new cycle. New challenges beckon and they can be approached with confidence. All things will be possible in the fullness of time.

THE MINOR ARCANA

While the cards in the Major Arcana deal with the archetypal stages and milestones in life, those in the Minor Arcana refer to the day-to-day activities, events and people in our lives and to experiences that have a short-term impact upon us.

The Minor Arcana is made up of the four suits – Wands, Cups, Swords and Pentacles. Each suit suit can be seen as a journey or cycle, similar to the story that unfolds with the Major Arcana. The suits begin with the ace and ascend in numerical order to ten, then the court cards.

The Court cards

There are sixteen court cards in the Tarot pack; each of the four suits has a king, a queen, a knight and a page.

If a court card appears in a spread, it may represent an individual in your life who possesses the card's particular attributes. However, it can also represent qualities of the querent which need to find expression.

The kings represent mature male authority figures who embody power, paternalism, achievement and responsibility. Queens are mature, maternal females and, like the kings, figures of authority. They embody wisdom, confidence, fertility and life-giving qualities. Knights are immature men and women who are rash in their actions and tend to pursue their own desires and interests at the expense of others. Knights indicate change and movement in a new direction. Pages refer to children or young teenagers of either gender and represent youthful potential, dreams and other characteristics that are hard to define. The qualities they embody are delicate and need to be nurtured if they are to develop. Pages are messengers and indicate that news of some kind will be received.

WANDS

Wands are associated with the element of fire and represent sparks of energy and the life force. They are represented by branches which are sprouting leaves, suggesting creation, regeneration and potential for the future. There is a great deal of energetic activity in the wands, which translates into action – sometimes creative and sometimes defensive or aggressive. Many wands in a spread indicate that events are moving quickly. Wands are sometimes referred to by

other names, including rods, staves, staffs and batons, depending on which deck of cards or book you use.

Ace of Wands

Keywords: beginning, change, opportunity, adventure, creativity, hope, action

The Ace of Wands signifies new beginnings and opportunities that can mark a change of direction in a person's life. There is the chance to embark on a journey or adventure, which may be sparked off by a new job opportunity, enterprise or relationship. The situation is full of hope and creative potential. It can also presage a birth in the family. Follow your intuition in taking up the right opportunities. Decide what you want to do and act quickly or you may miss your chance.

Two of Wands

Keywords: rest after hard work, patience, trust, planning for the future

The Two of Wands indicates that a new goal or project is on the horizon. It has taken courage, care and determination to formulate your plan, so now you can stand back and allow it to unfold and grow. Leaving the matter alone to allow the magic to work can lead to a period of restlessness. Patience and trust in the future are required. At this time you should make plans for the next stage and work out what to do once your creative endeavours have taken root and started to grow. Negotiations with others may be required. Travel may be indicated.

Three of Wands

Keywords: accomplishment, success, satisfaction, progression

The Three of Wands represents hopes and plans that have been realized in the world. As the image on the card suggests, your ships are sailing home and success is on the horizon. The first stage of a project has been completed and there is a feeling of great satisfaction and pride in your accomplishment. But remember there is much work ahead so you must not become complacent. Avoid arrogance and remember you have not always been this fortunate and could lose your fortune again. The momentum of your success may propel you into the next stage of your project or creative endeavour.

Four of Wands

Keywords: reward, blessing, celebration, happiness, harmony, romance

The Four of Wands suggests that you can reap the rewards of your achievements. The card promises a time of peace and harmony. It is a temporary calm before the storm – more hard work and energy will be required again soon to resolve problems and conflicts that will arise. But for the time being a great deal of satisfaction and celebration is in order. Be charming and amiable and enjoy sharing your success with others. Romance may be in the air.

Five of Wands

Keywords: fighting, conflict, obstacles, compromise.

The fives of each suit mark the crunch points along the journey. The Five of Wands suggests conflict, as demonstrated by the fight scene on the card. It can also indicate the possibility of lawsuits. In your effort to accomplish your goals you have had to make difficult decisions and possibly cut corners or stepped on other people's toes along the way. This may have been unavoidable, but now you must battle it out. Try not to compete, but find a way to resolve the matter; compromise, if necessary. You need to hammer out the problem and find a resolution. If you behave honourably, things could turn out to your advantage.

Six of Wands

Keywords: success, leadership, resolution, fortune, acclaim

In the Six of Wands, problems have been dealt with and a matter is on the point of being successfully resolved. You have the support of friends and colleagues in realising your aims. Good news is on the way, so don't give up now. You should stay true to your original vision and goals. The card may indicate that you will receive public acclaim for your activities and efforts. Exams will have a positive outcome. Relationships are about to take a turn for the better.

Seven of Wands

Keywords: upper hand, position of advantage, challenge, force, reassessment

With the Seven of Wands you face another battle with others, but this time you have the upper hand. Remember to play fair, but maintain control over a situation and keep applying force. In the process you will learn to harness your competitive instincts to defend yourself and your creative endeavours. The challenges you face can also help you to reassess your plans and goals and modify your behaviour as required. This will make you stronger and more successful in the long run.

Eight of Wands

Keywords: movement, progress, back on track, goals on their way to being achieved

The Eight of Wands represents a plan on its way to completion. You are back on track after a period of conflict and delay. Obstacles have been cleared and the way is free. You are focused on attaining your goals and forging ahead with your plans. Things are on the move. News may herald major changes in your life. Events are moving quickly and circumstances will soon change for the better. Things you hoped for will come to pass. Travel may be required to secure a matter in your favour.

Nine of Wands

Keywords: final challenge, goal in sight, perseverance, tenacity, determination, courage to overcome

The Nine of Wands represents last-minute challenges on your way to attaining a goal. You have come a long way and are determined not to give up now. Although it may not seem like it at the moment, what you have been hoping for is within reach. With your goal in sight, you find the courage and tenacity to give one final push. If you persevere, no obstacle can stand in your way for long. From deep within you must find the resources to keep going and remain hopeful. You have been given a final chance to prove you are worthy of success, it is up to you to rise to the challenge.

Ten of Wands

Keywords: achievement, attainment of goals, satisfaction, experience gained, rest and regeneration needed

In the Ten of Wands, an old man is reaching his final destination. He is hunched over with the weight of his load. You have come a long way and are weighed down with the responsibility of turning your vision into reality. Your efforts are about to pay off, but at a cost for you have been shaped by bitter experience and have lost the innocence and optimism of youth. As you reach the end of the cycle you can find satisfaction in all your achievements so far. You will need to rest and recharge your batteries so that new ideas can form and you can start the process again.

Page of Wands

Keywords: active, playful, imaginative, inspired, creative, youthful, folly

The Page of Wands is an active and boisterous youth with a fertile imagination. This card represents the urge to explore and play, to follow your dreams and look for new experiences and adventures. The Page seeks to avoid the responsibility that comes with maturity. When this card appears, it may represent a person, young or old, whose behaviour is eternally youthful. It may also represent your own need to break from stifling habits and responsibilities and develop these creative qualities within yourself.

Knight of Wands

Keywords: honourable, courageous, hasty, unreliable, aggressive, volatile, new direction

The Knight of Wands is a great warrior who loves to take risks and prove himself worthy. An honourable opponent, he defends the vulnerable and fights for their cause. He can be hot-headed and temperamental and may rush to conclusions. The card may describe someone you know who fits these characteristics or could indicate that you need to develop your warrior-like qualities to defend yourself or your loved ones. The Knight of Wands often signifies a move to a new home or a new direction in life.

Queen of Wands

Keywords: strong, courageous, generous, vibrant, creative, wise, intuitive

The Queen of Wands is a wise woman, independent and authoritative, imaginative and intuitive, strong and courageous. She knows what she wants and how to get it. The Queen makes a warm, lively host who is generous with her gifts. The card may describe a woman you know who fits these characteristics or may indicate that you need to develop these qualities yourself.

King of Wands

Keywords: intuitive, decisive, active, inspirational, visionary

The King of Wands is a mature man of vision who inspires others. He has strong leadership qualities and uses his wisdom and powers of intuition to guide him in decision-making. Sprightly and full of energy, the King engages with life to the full. The card could describe a man you know who fits these characteristics or indicate that you need to develop these qualities of leadership, activity and inspiration.

CUPS

Cups are associated with the element of water and represent feelings, love, relationships and emotional fulfilment. They also signify the vast imaginative reserves within us and our unconscious realm. Water quenches our thirst and brings satisfaction and fulfillment.

The cups themselves are vessels for holding water and they are often full (indicating fulfillment); however, sometimes the water is spilt (indicating crisis and sorrow) or overflowing (suggesting abundance). Many cups in a spread signify that feelings and relationships are highlighted. The cups are sometimes referred to by other names, including chalices, goblets and cauldrons, depending on which deck of cards or book you use.

Ace of Cups

Keywords: love, joy, happiness, abundance, relationship, emotional expression, fertility

The Ace of Cups, like the overflowing waters pictured on the card, indicates freely flowing emotions which need to find expression. There is potential for great emotional fulfillment. Deeply satisfying love and happiness are possible. The Ace of Cups represents the start of a new relationship or it can indicate a marriage proposal. There is the chance of a fresh start and a new lease of life. There is great hope for the future – your emotions will sustain you and love will find a way!

Two of Cups

Keywords: new relationship, attraction, romance, harmony, satisfaction, conception, emotional fulfillment

The Two of Cups heralds the start of a new relationship, romantic attraction or connection with another person. You have the capacity for deep satisfaction and fulfillment. It feels as though you have met your match in another person. You see yourself reflected and mirrored back by your partner and find out about new aspects of your character through his or her eyes. Existing relationships are strengthened. The card can indicate a marriage union or conception of a child or another creative endeavour.

Three of Cups

Keywords: pleasure, joy, marriage, birth, feasting, merriment, celebration, abundance, fortune

The Three of Cups indicates that there will be a happy gathering of people. This card may herald a pregnancy or marriage proposal or success in a creative endeavour close to your heart. You can be proud of your achievements. Joy and cause for celebration are indicated. This is a time to share your good fortune with others. You have renewed faith in the power of love.

Four of Cups

Keywords: dissatisfaction, boredom, discontent, depression, crisis, re-evaluation, self-questioning

In the image on the Four of Cups card a young man ignores the three cups he already has and the one being offered to him. For some reason you feel unhappy and discontented with your lot. You are in danger of developing a careless attitude towards life and becoming apathetic. You are entering a period of personal crisis and questioning and you have temporarily lost your connection with loved ones. You may feel that something is lost or missing from your life. The card indicates that you don't realise how fortunate you are. You need to take time to re-evaluate rour life and decide what is really important to you.

Five of Cups

Keywords: loss, sorrow, regret, despair, betrayal, neglect, emotional breakdown, relationship breakup

The Five of Cups can presage a relationship or marriage breakup. The image on the card shows a man in a black cloak turning his back and withdrawing from the world. Three cups have been spilled on the ground, indicating relationships that have been lost or thrown away. However, two full cups remain: this means you have a chance to hold on to whatever is left. You should think carefully before coming to a decision, for the effect could have consequences for yourself and your loved ones.

Six of Cups

Keywords: calm, serenity, acceptance, simple pleasures, nostalgia, old friends, new hope and opportunity

The Six of Cups is the calm after an emotional storm. Although things might not be perfect, you learn to accept your limits and find a new appreciation of those close to you and with whom you share your life. Your thoughts may be focused on the past and you may start to idealise the 'good times' as you remember them. An old friend may re-enter your life and help you come to terms with what you have become, bringing a fresh opportunity and a new lease of life. New friendships can also blossom. Hope in the future will be renewed.

Seven of Cups

Keywords: decision, choice, dream, vision, imagination, new path

The Seven of Cups suggests you are at a crossroads in life or in a particular matter. You have a very important decision to make and there appears to be more than one option open to you. In this card you see the cups situated in rows in the clouds. Each cup is filled with a different magical item. You may rely on the imagination, a dream or a vision to choose the right path. But you are advised to remain grounded and realistic when working with the imaginary realm or your decisions will be short-lived and you won't be able to stick with them for long.

Eight of Cups

Keywords: retreat, escape, abandonment, loss, dissatisfaction, time out, perspective needed

The Eight of Cups indicates that you may need to go away for a while to work out what is really important to you. You are unfulfilled and dissatisfied with your choices and find it difficult to choose something and stick with it. Nothing seems to bring the satisfaction for which you are yearning. You must find a way to gain some perspective on your life before deciding what to do next. The card can indicate that the time has come to move on. You may need to find a way to let something go and trust that things are on the right track. You may also need to lose something for a while before it comes back.

Nine of Cups

Keywords: wishes fulfilled, hopes realised, positive outcome, childbirth, joy, success, reward

The Nine of Cups is known as the 'nine months card' and indicates the birth of a baby or another creative endeavour. Something you have tended and nurtured has come to fruition. You are brimming with joy and the

world is filled with hope again. Health and happiness are offered and the problems of the past have evaporated. A wish will be fulfilled and things will work out unexpectedly well. You can enjoy your good fortune and find satisfaction in what you have achieved.

Ten of Cups

Keywords: lasting happiness, joy, fulfillment, emotional stability, fortunate outcome

The Ten of Cups is a card of emotional security and long-lasting fortune in matters of the heart. More happiness than you might have thought possible will be yours. The card indicates you have met, or will meet, the person with whom you want to spend the rest of your life. A situation has the best possible outcome. A stable, lasting relationship and family life are indicated. You can relax and enjoy the rewards of your efforts and good fortune.

The Page of Cups

Keywords: sensitive, sympathetic, kind, imaginative, poetic, lazy, daydreamer

The Page of Cups is a sensitive youth – a kind, generous soul who is easily hurt, feels other people's pain and is sympathetic to their needs. The Page may be naturally lazy at times and prone to daydreaming. He needs plenty of space to play and explore the imaginative realm. He or she may be oversensitive and may not take criticism well. News from a loved one could be indicated. This card may suggest a character who displays these qualities, or infer that these characteristics need to be developed within ourselves.

The Knight of Cups

Keywords: romantic, chivalrous, idealistic, questing, highly principled, on a mission

The Knight of Cups is the knight in shining armour of the pack, in all his romantic splendour. He rides around the kingdom searching for his love, ready to save her from any misfortune and ride off with her into the sunset. The Knight may also be on another quest – to seek the Holy Grail and restore the health of the King, bringing balance, peace and harmony to the kingdom.

This card may describe a chivalrous young man or woman with a sense of mission and high ideals or it may highlight these characteristics within ourselves.

The Queen of Cups

Keywords: emotional, sensitive, caring, peace-loving, harmonious, imaginative, creative talents

The Queen of Cups is in touch with her feelings. Wise and peace-loving, she is in tune with others. She is sensitive, sympathetic and kind-hearted. A good listener, she can advise others on matters that are causing concern. The Queen is a highly imaginative woman with creative gifts and talents. This card can represent a mature woman with these characterstics or it can refer to these qualities in your own character.

The King of Cups

Keywords: kind, honourable, responsible, respected, considerate, easily swayed

The King of Cups is a kind, honourable male who is trusted and respected by others. He is naturally caring and puts the needs of his subjects first. A just and fair ruler, he has earned the respect of others. He can be easily swayed and manipulated, however, so may become distrustful of others' motives. This card can be chosen to represent an individual with these qualities, or it may highlight these tendencies within ourselves.

SWORDS

Swords are associated with the element of air and represent ideas, rational thought and communication. They concern the ideals of truth and justice. The swords are active principles and the cards describe circumstances in which you are called to fight for what you believe in. Their blades are notoriously double-edged, indicating that every decision you make or ideal you support may have both beneficial and harmful consequences. Swords are made of cold, hard metal, suggesting a lack of feeling or emotion. A number of swords in a spread indicates a focus on thinking – you may be called to fight for or be forced to reconsider your beliefs and ideals. Swords

are sometimes referred to by other names, including daggers, knives and blades, depending on which deck of cards or book you use.

Ace of Swords

Keywords: beginning, hope, ideals, principles, justice, conquest, new direction

The Ace of Swords stands for your principles and ideals. You have decided to embark on a new life or take a new direction and have high expectations of your future. Justice will be done. You do not wish to compromise your strongly held beliefs. The card may indicate the birth of a child, bringing great hope for the future. You are asked to have faith in yourself and your ability to overcome any challenges that lie ahead.

Two of Swords

Keywords: tension, balance, stalemate, difficult decision, action needed

The Two of Swords indicates that a matter is in the balance and a difficult decision must be made. You cannot decide between two options open to you. The figure in the image on the card is blindfolded, suggesting that the way ahead is obscured. You must make a decision and stick by it. You should act now and not allow fears and doubts to hold you back. The sooner you make a decision, the sooner you can move on and find relief from a situation that is hanging over you.

Three of Swords

Keywords: conflict, struggle, heartache, disappointment, arguments, tears, separation

The Three of Swords has the stark image of a heart with three swords passed through it. This card suggests the experience of pain and disappointment in matters of the heart, perhaps because of a love triangle. Feelings may be sacrificed in the interest of rational thinking. Quarrels and squabbles with loved ones are indicated. A separation of some kind may result. In gaining some distance from the matter you will find relief and realise that change was necessary in the long run.

Four of Swords

Keywords: rest, retreat, withdrawal, recuperation, relief from anxieties, rebuilding strength

The Four of Swords offers solace from a matter that has caused anguish. The card shows the tomb of a knight in a church; the effigy has his hands clasped in prayer. Something has been lost and part of you feels as though it has died with it. You need time alone to contemplate what has happened and where things might have gone wrong. You must rebuild your strength and reorganise your thoughts before you are ready to face the world again.

Five of Swords

Keywords: unfair play, dishonour, belligerence, loss, facing consequences

The Five of Swords indicates unfair play and belligerent actions without consideration of their effects in the long run. You may have the upper hand in a matter, but your victory is double-edged and causes as much sorrow to you as it does to your adversaries. You have acted dishonourably and disobeyed authority to gain the upper hand. You must swallow your pride and approach a situation honestly and be prepared to face the consequences of your actions.

Six of Swords

Keywords: solace, respite, retreat, healing, journey, insight, reputation restored

The Six of Swords may suggest that every ounce of strength has been sapped from you following a tough time, but the worst has now passed. The card indicates that a journey might be the best way to resolve a matter; this may be a journey in the literal sense or a journey of the mind. You are confronted with your subconscious thoughts and, as a result, insights may arise. You should allow things to sort themselves out without intervening. A matter that has been causing you great concern is on its way to being resolved.

Seven of Swords

Keywords: cunning, guile, deceit, tact, diplomacy, flexibility, compromise for the greater good

The Seven of Swords indicates that a situation calls for you to behave falsely in order to attain positive results. The card shows a figure stealing swords from a military camp. While such an act may be dishonourable and your personal principles may be compromised, your actions may be necessary for the greater good. This card suggests there are times when your beliefs and ideals must be flexible and you should adapt them to the task at hand. Life throws many situations at us and we can't afford to be too rigid in our thinking when we come to deal with them.

Eight of Swords

Keywords: restriction, mistrust, inability to act, indecision, imprisonment, isolation from others

The Eight of Swords represents restriction and mistrust. Like the Two of Swords, the figure in this card is blindfolded and afraid to act and face the consequences. But the figure on the Eight of Swords is bound and surrounded by a wall of swords, as if held in a prison. A situation seems hopeless and you can't see a way out. You have run out of excuses and of ways to avoid making a decision – there is no escape. You must learn to trust others and should not be afraid to ask for help. You need to rebuild your connection with others and end your isolation before a decision is possible.

Nine of Swords

Keywords: fear, doubt, anxiety, nightmares, troubled conscience, suffering, despair

The Nine of Swords represents great anxiety and suffering. The figure depicted on the card is in bed but unable to sleep; she holds her head in despair. Your hopes have been dashed, you are filled with fear and doubt and you struggle to come to terms with a matter. You blame yourself for an unfortunate outcome, but need to keep things in perspective. While it is necessary to face your part in a situation, you are only human and will make mistakes. You need to forgive and accept your limitations before you can lay the past to rest and move on.

Ten of Swords

Keywords: endings, misfortune, loss, defeat, new understanding, fresh perspective

The Ten of Swords represents defeat and marks the end of a difficult matter. The image on the card is of a man lying on the ground with ten swords in his back. At the end of a long struggle, something has been irrevocably lost. You must put the past behind you and move on to the next stage of the cycle. While you have been defeated on this occasion, lessons have been learned and you will move on with a new understanding of yourself and a fresh perspective.

Page of Swords

Keywords: curiosity, intelligence, wit, honesty, independence, clash with authority

The Page of Swords is a clever, witty youth with a natural curiosity and inquisitive nature. He is in the process of developing his own ideas and beliefs and may frequently clash with authority over differences of opinion. The youth's independent ideas and curious spirit should be encouraged and nurtured rather than quashed. This card may represent a boy or girl who displays these qualities or may suggest that such gifts should be developed by the querent.

Knight of Swords

Keywords: fighter, warrior, reformer, prepared to make sacrifices for just causes

The Knight of Swords is a brave warrior who fights for the causes he believes in and is charged to protect. The Knight challenges injustice wherever he sees it and shows courage against all odds. He is willing to make sacrifices to uphold his principles and fights for justice, fairness and reform. Change will be brought about. This card may represent a young man or woman who displays these qualities or could suggest the time is right for the querent to develop such characteristics.

Queen of Swords

Keywords: just, fair, intelligent, faithful, warrior, strong beliefs, idealistic, highly principled.

The Queen of Swords has a strong mind and keen intelligence. With a cool exterior, she may sometimes seem icy or aloof, but she is always kind and fair toward her subjects. The Queen will argue her opinions with a clear head and keen insight. She is not afraid to fight for her principles if her duties require it. When this card is selected, it may represent a female who displays these qualities or may indicate the time is right for these characteristics to be developed by the querent.

King of Swords

Keywords: intelligent, logical, fair, law-maker, judge, counsellor, warrior, strategist

The King of Swords is intelligent and known for his keen sense of logic and clear-headedness. He is an excellent judge and counsellor to his people and a capable warrior and military strategist. He has many innovative ideas, encourages reform and change and runs an orderly, civilised society. When this card is selected, it may represent a man who displays these qualities or could suggest that they should be developed by the querent.

KING of SWORDS

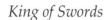

PENTACLES

Pentacles are associated with the element of earth and represent matter, the body and the physical world. Pentacles are concerned with material security and finances as well as personal values and the sense of security that comes from within. This suit also represents physical health and wellbeing and the ability to draw comfort and satisfaction from personal possessions and the physical world. The pentacles themselves are in the shape of coins, suggesting money and earnings. Another word for money is talent; the pentacles represent talents and abilities that help us earn money and contribute to society in a useful way. Many pentacles in a spread suggest that material gain is highlighted in a matter and practical action may be required. The pentacles are sometimes referred to by other names, including coins and discs, depending on which deck of cards or book you use.

Ace of Pentacles

Keywords: new venture, opportunity, promise of wealth, achievement

The Ace of Pentacles suggests a new opportunity or venture that will put our innate talents to good use. Like the other aces, this card represents high hopes for success and an opportunity to make something of our talents, provided we use them wisely.

Two of Pentacles

Keywords: balance, weighing up pros and cons, careful consideration, common sense, responsible decision-making

The Two of Pentacles is concerned with juggling or balancing two different duties, weighing up the pros and cons of a matter and making a carefully considered decision. In the image on the card the figure balances two pentacles that are connected by the symbol of a cosmic lemiscate. This indicates that the figure must keep all his responsibilities in balance. If he fails to do so, he will be forced to drop one of the pentacles and the harmony between them will be destroyed. Behind the figure, ships sail on the ocean, but the rolling waves suggest that emotional imbalances affect your stability in the material realm. Under the circumstances, you are challenged to make the most practical choice you can.

Three of Pentacles

Keywords: craftsperson, skilled artisan, recognition of abilities, achievement

The Three of Pentacles indicates that you will be recognised for your skills and achievements. Your handiwork is appreciated by others. You have worked hard and earned your success so far. While establishing a new venture you have honed your

skills and built a good reputation. Now you must reassess your goals and develop in a new direction You can start another project from a position of strength. Financial affairs will blossom.

Four of Pentacles

Keywords: thrift, over-protectiveness, lack of generosity, mistrust, paranoia, isolation

The Four of Pentacles represents a withholding, ungenerous nature. You are afraid of losing what you have gained, so you hold on tightly to everything to prevent it being snatched away. You begin to become paranoid about other people's motives and are so afraid of losing what you have that you lose touch with others and become unapproachable. This card can indicate a tendency toward obsessive compulsive behaviour, hypochondria and a fear of taking risks. It warns that self-imposed isolation and the desire for total control mean you are detached from the wider world and in danger of pushing away those who love you.

Five of Pentacles

Keywords: financial worries, fear of loss, destitution, failure, shame, re-evaluation, starting again

The Five of Pentacles indicates financial worries and fear of loss or failure. The image on the card shows two destitute figures outside a church, suggesting both material and spiritual impoverishment. The card may presage the failure of a venture, loss of a job or redundancy. You feel you have not lived up to your high standards and expectations. Your fear of loss may have led to this situation. You must reassess your behaviour and regain faith in your talents and abilities. You have the capacity to work hard, rebuild your reputation and achieve your ambitions.

Six of Pentacles

Keywords: success, sharing of wealth, charity, philanthropy, giving back to society

The Six of Pentacles signifies the sharing of good fortune with others. You have learned the lesson of the previous cards and now understand the consequence of holding on to too tightly to material possessions. Plans are working out, you have succeeded in rebuilding your reputation in the world and can celebrate your success with others. Much satisfaction is gained from sharing time and money with worthy causes.

Seven of Pentacles

Keywords: rest after work, disappointing returns, re-evaluation of projects, redirecting efforts

The Seven of Pentacles indicates weariness after a period of hard work and suggests pausing to assess what you have achieved so far. It asks you to re-evaluate your plans and take stock of a situation. Are you on the best route to success? Perhaps you are overworked and disappointed with the rewards of your labours. A period of recuperation and regeneration may be necessary and you might want to take a short break if you can afford it. You should not lose faith, but pick yourself up again and implement the improvements that are needed.

Eight of Pentacles

Keywords: new skills, apprenticeship, confidence, job satisfaction, reward

The Eight of Pentacles represents learning a new skill. You may be training in a new trade fairly late in life. You are slowly but surely gaining mastery in your work and can reap the rewards of your efforts so far. Financial gain and job satisfaction are indicated. Faith in your skills and confidence that you will achieve your ambitions will help you stay on the right path.

Nine of Pentacles

Keywords: pleasure, self-esteem, humility, realistic evaluation, sense of achievement, satisfaction, windfall

The Nine of Pentacles indicates that you can take pleasure and satisfaction in your work and reap the rewards of your labours. You have worked hard to develop your talents and abilities and have proved yourself a capable and worthy member of society. You are realistic about your limitations and

recognise that you have had failures along the way. However, you can be proud of everything you have achieved so far and can draw great satisfaction from recognising where you have come from and what you have been through to get where you are today. An inheritance or unexpected windfall might be indicated by this card.

Ten of Pentacles

Keywords: security, inheritance, lasting success, satisfaction, sharing, rewards, contentment

The Ten of Pentacles indicates that lasting success and material satisfaction have been achieved. You have earned the right to relax and enjoy what has been accumulated through your efforts. The card suggests that you have also gained an inner sense of security. In addition to your personal wealth, a family inheritance may ensure that you live in comfort for a long time. Enjoying the company of your family and loved ones and sharing your material fortune with them brings the greatest pleasure now. The card indicates a satisfying home life and the chance to pass on a positive inheritance to your descendants.

Page of Pentacles

Keywords: diligent, reliable, mature, loyal, steady, hardworking, responsible

The Page of Pentacles is mature beyond his years and is the type of youth you can depend on – reliable and hard working in his studies and keen to start working from an early age. The Page of Pentacles makes a loyal, steady friend. A message about money may be received. The Page may represent a youthful person who displays these qualities or may highlight the need to nurture these qualities in ourselves.

Knight of Pentacles

Keywords: sensible, considerate, stable, responsible, respectful, practical, nervous

The Knight of Pentacles is a practical, sensible, considerate character, with a strong sense of duty and respect for others. Unlike the other knights, the Knight of Pentacles acts with caution, taking care not to rock the boat. Knights are normally very active principles who fight for change of some sort. This knight needs to find a way of balancing these two tendencies or they will pull in different directions and lead to nervous tension. This card may represent a young man or woman known for these qualities, or may indicate the need to develop them in our own characters.

Queen of Pentacles

Keywords: generous stable, sensible, down-to-earth, warm, comforting, healthy, contented

The Queen of Pentacles is practical, down-to-earth and generous with her gifts. She has an affinity with nature and animals and radiates comfort and confidence in her body. She enjoys tending to her surroundings and taking care of others. She can be relied upon to give fair, sensible advice and find practical solutions to problems. This card may represent a mature woman who displays these qualities or can highlight the need to develop them in ourselves.

King of Pentacles

Keywords: sensible, fair, honest, patient, generous, practical, traditional, stable, humble, self-reliant

The King of Pentacles is an honest, generous leader who has worked hard and achieved great success. He upholds his duties and traditions and respects his ancestral heritage. The King finds practical solutions to problems and dislikes experimenting with new methods and technologies, preferring the old way of doing things. The King is kind, but has high expectations of others and expects them to have the same self-discipline and work ethic that he has. He is humble and self-reliant. This card can represent a mature man who displays these qualities or can indicate the need to recognise them in ourselves.

FORTUNE-TELLING
WITH
PLAYING CARDS

REGULAR PLAYING CARDS can be used to divine the future in a similar way to Tarot cards. The meanings of the playing cards correspond roughly with those of the Minor Arcana in the Tarot. However, while there are four court cards in the Tarot (Page, Knight, Queen and King), there are only three in a pack of playing cards (Jack, Queen, King). Therefore the Jack in the playing cards is treated as a combination of the Page and the Knight in the Tarot deck.

ORIGINS

The earliest set of playing cards was discovered in China and dates back to the ninth century. However, there is evidence that the Pharoahs and historical figures through the ages consulted card readers. According to legend, Napoleon is thought to have used the power of the pack to divine the right moment to mount his military campaigns. In a modern deck, the court cards show figures wearing clothes dating back to fourteenth century Europe, when playing cards became popular across the continent.

There are numerous different types of playing cards in popular use today; there are even variations among European cards. In France, the cards are slightly different from the UK deck, although the four suits remain the same. However, in Italy, Spain, Germany and Switzerland the packs are quite dissimilar. In Switzerland and Germany, clubs are known as acorns and diamonds are called bells. In Switzerland, spades are flowers and hearts are shields. In Germany, spades are leaves and hearts are the same as in the UK. In Italy and Spain, clubs are called swords, diamonds are coins, spades are batons and hearts are cups.

Whatever the differences in nomenclature, any deck of cards can be used to divine the future. As with the Tarot, playing cards can be used to answer a simple question or give a more in-depth reading. According to tradition, Tarot cards consulted for divination should not be used for any other purpose and should be stored carefully wrapped in a protective cloth or pouch. It is not essential to store playing cards in this way, but if you wish to use them for fortune-telling it is advisable to treat them with the same respect as you would the Tarot.

If the reading is for someone other than yourself, shuffle the pack first and give it to the querent to shuffle again (some say you should pass the card from your left hand to the querent's left hand but, as usual, let instinct be your guide). Ask the querent to cut the pack three times, again with the left hand, then take the cards and spread them out, face down, in a row with the cards overlapping one another. Now select the cards to be read at random and place them in a spread. You can use the same spreads as the ones in the Tarot readings (see previous chapter).

Turn the cards over one by one and read them in the order in which they were laid down, using your instinct and experience to glean their meanings. Remember that all the cards in the spread have some kind of connection with one another and tell a particular story.

THE MEANING OF THE PLAYING CARDS

The meaning of each playing card is related to its corresponding Tarot card (see Table of Correspondences and Meanings on pages 64–67). Like the Tarot, the significance of each card depends on the question being asked and the context of the matter as well as the card's position in the spread. Therefore the individual meanings of the cards should be learnt and applied to the context of the reading.

Unlike the Tarot, however, certain combinations of cards in a spread have specific meanings. For example, a Jack next to a King or a Queen indicates protection; the Ten of Hearts next to the Ace of Diamonds indicates a blossoming romance that may lead to marriage; the Ten of Spades next to any ace warns of danger.

Multiple cards of the same number have particular significance. For example, two aces next to each other indicate partnerships or marriage proposals. However, if there are one or more cards between them in the spread this suggests that others will come between the two individuals. Three aces anywhere in the spread suggests good news and four aces indicates victory in a matter.

As is customary, the Ace is the highest card in value and importance (its value is both 1 and 11). In 'yes or no' questions, an Ace can indicate that the answer is 'yes'.

The two joker cards in the deck can be used as wild cards and represent an element of fate or of outside forces intervening in a matter. The jokers perform a similar role to that of the Major Arcana cards in the Tarot (in particular, the Fool, the Magician and the Wheel of Fortune). When a joker appears in a spread it indicates that we are not in control of a matter and the direction in which things are heading has not been decided and may be reversed.

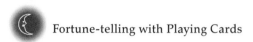

PLAYING CARDS: TABLE OF CORRESPONDENCES AND MEANINGS

	GENERAL MEANING	CLUBS	HEARTS
Tarot suit		Wands	Cups
Element		Fire	Water
General meaning		Hopes, dreams, projects, journeys, travel, energy, expansion	Love, romance, feelings, emotions, relationships, partnerships
Ace	New beginnings	New path; the start of a project or a journey; creative venture, wealth, excitement	The start of a partnership or the birth of a child, new hope for the future
2	Duality, partnership, opposition	Challenges, obstacles, disappointment, mistrust in relationships, desire for freedom and independence	Successful relationships, possible marriage; bridges built and quarrels mended
3	Harmony	Attracting money, success and good fortune through a partnership or marriage; luck	Harmony in relationships; commitment problems, possible love triangle; indecision
4	Stability, consolidation	Dissatisfaction, sense of restriction; being held back by responsibilities or let down by others	Restlessness and lack of satisfaction in relationships; a choice must be made
5	Conflict	Argument, anger, self-defence, ill health, possible accidents, fiery relationships; obstacles must be overcome in order to progress	Temporary misunderstandings and jealousy cloud the way forward; acceptance of a matter is required
6	Temporary resolution, acceptance	Time to take a break and recharge your batteries; regain strength and energy before moving forward	Harmony in love, family and friendship, positive influences, good news

SPADES	DIAMONDS
Spades	Pentacles
Air	Earth
Ideas, intellect, reason, communication, truth, justice, peace, harmony	Money, value, security, duty, ambition, business, practical matters
Embarking on a quest, a romance, artistic creation that will change your life, a discovery	New business opportunity, new idea; receipt of news purchasing a property, apprenticeship, health, prosperity
Logic required to resolve a matter; choosing between unappealing alternatives	Successful business relationship, possible material gain through marriage partnership
Use reason and communication to sweep rivals aside; truth and honesty are required	Extra commitments will be worth while in the long term; possible quarrels and legal disputes
Loneliness and regret; self-reflection and a renewed sense of determination are required	Material security, solid foundations, plans taking root, stability in home life
Temporary delays; dishonest and spiteful actions prevent progress; loneliness and disillusionment are indicated	Responsibilities weighing down on a heavy heart, health problems a temporary setback; diligence is required
A time for self-reflection; problems are resolved and help received from an unexpected source	Caution in financial affairs is advised; a time to focus on home matters

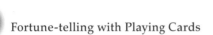

	GENERAL MEANING	CLUBS	HEARTS
7	Surprise turn of events	Personal success, new hope and encouragement to achieve your dreams	Broken promises, disappointment; trust your instincts and allow dreams and signs to guide you
8	Reward, inheritance	Opportunities arise and should be grabbed quickly, beware of greed and hubris	A celebration is indicated; be wary of jealousy arising from insecurity
9	Hopes and expectations	Crisis of faith, self-doubt, reassessment of plans and goals; possibility of a sudden windfall	Hopes and wishes for the future on the brink of being realised
10	Achievement, completion	The end of a journey, successful achievement of goals; good fortune, hopes and dreams realised	Happy marriage or union; emotional fulfillment through sharing with others; birth, new beginning, full of promise
Jack	Young boy or girl	Energetic, active, risk-taking, adventurous; can be fickle	Sensitive, tender-hearted, imaginative; can be a day-dreamer and lack realistic goals and ambitions
Queen	Mature woman	Generous, kind, joyful, lively and sociable; may be tactless and overbearing	Affectionate, caring, compassionate; can tend to place the welfare of others above her own
King	Mature man	Successful, confident, ambitious, innovative; may be impatient and insensitive towards others	Artistic and romantic; in touch with imagination and emotions; may be passive and lacking in leadership

SPADES	DIAMONDS
Conflict and sorrow are indicated; possible betrayal; stick to what you believe to be right and justice will prevail	Stability in financial matters; new opportunites arise, possible promotion
Frustration, things not going to plan; effort is required to overcome fears and doubts	Discovery of a new talent or interest that will attract wealth and fortune
Fear of failure and rejection; need to regain confidence and determination to achieve goals	Taking stock, assessing what remains to be done to achieve your aims
Ideals and expectations realised; possible disappointment, bad news or worry; a new start with more realistic expectations beckons	Material success, plans realised, deep sense of satisfaction and contentment, sensual pleasures
Intelligent, studious; full of hopes and dreams for the future; may be unrealistic and overly idealistic	Reliable, realistic, ambitious; full of common sense; may be mature beyond his or her years
Intelligent, calm woman; may have high ideals and expectations that are inevitably disappointed	Kind, helpful, practical and organised; may be overly realistic and cynical
Progressive, intellectual, objective, fair-minded; may be emotionally distant and reserved	Responsible, reliable, prosperous, patient, wise; may be old-fashioned and afraid of change

TASSEOGRAPHY

Tasseography, from the Arabic word *tassa*, meaning 'cup', refers to the practice of reading the symbols formed by sediments in a cup. The most popular forms of tasseography today are the practices of tea-leaf and coffee-ground reading. Other forms include reading the sediments left by wine or herbal remedies, both of which were popular in ancient times.

TEA-LEAF READING

Tea-leaf reading is often associated with Romany folk tradition. However, its history can be traced even further back, to before Confucius' time, when tea was revered for its rejuvenating properties in the tea-growing regions of China and the surrounding lands.

THE ORIGINS OF TEA-LEAF READING

By around 200 BC, tea drinking had become popular in China. According to one of many tea-related legends, it was discovered by the mythical Emperor Shen Nung. One day, while sitting beneath a wild tea tree, the Emperor boiled some water to drink. Several leaves fell from the tree into the water. The Emperor tasted the hot brew and enjoyed it so much that he introduced it to his court. So tea drinking began, spreading through the Far East and India and making its way to Europe in the sixteenth century. It did not become popular in Britain until the eighteenth century, when it began to be served in the coffee houses of the day. At this point, tea was in relatively short supply in Britain, so high taxes were introduced, turning it into an expensive commodity. It was so expensive that it was locked away in tea caddies. Finally, during the nineteenth century, traders began to import large quantities of tea from India and Ceylon (present-day Sri Lanka) in purpose-built ships.

While tea leaves were a late arrival to Britain and the rest of the world, herbal infusions had been popular since ancient times and were probably used for divination purposes in the same way that tea leaves are used today.

PREPARING FOR A TEA-LEAF READING

The methods used in tea-leaf reading vary from reader to reader. Some tasseographers like to use a white or plain coloured cup and saucer so that the

tea leaves are clearly visible. Others like to use cups with patterns which can assist with the interpretation – there are teacups made with special markings to help guide the reader in making an interpretation.

There are many different ways to practice tea-leaf reading, but the reader can follow these general steps:

1　Choose a good quality, loose-leaf tea – whichever kind you prefer to drink – and place one teaspoonful per person in a teapot (adjust the amount according to taste). Fill the pot with boiling water and leave to stand.

2　While the tea is brewing, the querent should decide on the question he or she wants to ask.

3　When the brew is the required strength, pour it into the teacups without using a strainer so that the leaves are released along with the liquid. Add milk and sugar to taste and enjoy drinking the tea – don't rush, just sip as usual. The querent may want to ponder his or her question while doing this.

4　When the tea is finished there should be a small amount of liquid left in the bottom of the cups, along with the tea leaves. The querent should swirl the cup three times with his or her left hand – clockwise for a question about the future; anti-clockwise for a question concerning the past.

5　The querent should now turn the cup over quickly, placing it upside down on the saucer to drain away any liquid that remains.

6　The reader concentrates on the question being asked before taking the cup in his or her left hand and proceeding to interpret the patterns made by the tea leaves.

READING THE LEAVES

As with other methods of divination, it is important to let instinct be your guide when reading tea leaves. First try to get a general impression from the position of the leaves in the cup. Then study the shapes that appear and think what they might signify – for this you will need to trust your imagination and intuition to guide you.

In addition to the shapes made by the leaves, you need to consider their size, clarity and position in the cup. The stronger and larger an image, the greater its significance. If a shape that can be discerned when the cup is first turned over slowly fades away, this indicates that a matter will be short-lived. The absence of tea leaves in certain parts of the cup also holds significance as it indicates that these realms are not relevant to the matter.

The cup is divided into quarters:

1 The quarter nearest the handle represents the querent. Leaves in this part of the cup relate to the querent's home and those people closest to him or her. If a large number of leaves stick to this part of the cup it could suggest that the querent is overwhelmed by responsibility for family and close friends or it could mean that home and personal life are particularly rich.

2 The quarter opposite the handle is concerned with strangers, acquaintances, the workplace, travel and other matters away from home. A large concentration of tea leaves in this quarter suggests that these matters dominate the querent's life at the moment, more than family and home.

3 To the left of the handle (from the seer's angle) is the area representing the past. Large deposits of tea leaves here indicate that unresolved matters have a bearing on the questioner's life at the moment.

4 The quarter of the cup to the right of the handle represents future events and people who are about to have an influence on the querent's life. An absence of leaves in this area indicates that the questioner is more concerned with the present and/or past at the moment.

The cup can also be divided into halves – the bottom half of the cup and the top half, close to the rim.

The top half and rim of the cup indicate the present and short-term, including days and weeks. If the quarters reading concerns the past, the top

half indicates the recent past. If the quarters reading concerns the future, the top half represents the near future. The rim is associated with happiness.

The lower half of the cup represents the long-term, including months and years. If the quarters reading concerns the past, the bottom half indicates the distant past. If the quarters reading concerns the future, the bottom half of the cup represents the distant future. The bottom of the cup is associated with problems and challenges.

COFFEE-GROUNDS READING

Coffee-grounds reading employs similar methods to tea-leaf reading. It is widely practised in the Middle East and Mediterranean, where it is a popular tradition passed down the generations, mainly by women.

THE ORIGINS OF COFFEE-GROUNDS READING

Originally cultivated in Ethiopia and Yemen, it is believed that coffee beans were first used to make a beverage in the sixth century. At first the beans were used in their raw state, but by the thirteenth century people had started to roast them to achieve a richer taste. The popularity of coffee as a drink, and its use in fortune telling, spread throughout the Middle East from the eleventh century onwards. However, it did not become widespread in Europe and North America until the eighteenth century.

PREPARING FOR A COFFEE-GROUNDS READING

Traditionally, coffee is prepared for readings using a special pan which has a wide bottom, narrow top and long handle. As with tea-leaf reading, there are various methods of divination, but the reader can follow these general steps:

1 Choose a good-quality, finely ground coffee – whichever type you prefer. If a traditional Middle-Eastern coffee pan is not available, use a cafetiere. Place one heaped teaspoonful of coffee per person in the cafetiere (adjust the amount as preferred). Fill with recently boiled water and leave to stand.

2 While the coffee is brewing, the querent decides on the question he or she wants to ask.

3 When the brew is the required strength, the reader stirs the coffee and pours it into a cup without using a strainer so that the grounds are released along with the liquid. He or she then adds milk and sugar to taste. The querent may want to ponder his or her question while drinking the coffee.

4 After the coffee has been drunk, a small amount of liquid should remain along with the sediment in the bottom of the cup. The querent now places the saucer upside-down over the cup and swirls them three times – in a clockwise direction for questions about the future, and anti-clockwise for questions about the past.

5 The querent then quickly places the cup and saucer upside down to drain away any remaining liquid and leaves them to cool and dry in this position for a few minutes.

6 The reader checks to see if the sediment has stuck to the sides of the cup. If it has, the reader concentrates on the question being asked before removing the cup from the saucer and turning it the right way up to start the reading.

READING THE COFFEE GROUNDS

If the cup is stuck firmly to the saucer, this is an early indication of good fortune and a positive outcome in the matter for the querent. A cup that is not stuck to the saucer does not mean the opposite – it is merely neutral and nothing to be concerned about.

Now the reader studies the position of the grounds in the cup. As with the tea-leaf reading, the cup can be divided into quarters and into top and bottom halves, each section representing a different sphere of life. The shapes made by the coffee grounds and the spaces between them where the ceramic of the cup is visible are interpreted by the reader. As a rule, shapes made by the coffee grounds are thought to be difficult influences, and shapes made by the spaces between the grounds represent beneficial influences. Reading the shapes can take some practice. The reader looks for

abstractions rather than for clearly defined images, allowing the imagination to wander as he or she peers into the cup and concentrates on the question. If no images are visible, the reader should turn the cup and look at it from another angle. Soon the images will start to form and their story will emerge.

The images in the cup should be read together to give an overall picture of the matter. As with tea leaves, the size, clarity and position of each shape needs to be taken into consideration along with the meaning of the images themselves.

AN A–Z OF SHAPES

Once you have ascertained the shapes made by the tea leaves or coffee grounds, you then need to work out their meanings. What follows is a guide to some of the most commonly discerned symbols in the cup. As with all symbols, the shapes can mean different things to different readers. To one tasseographer, an acorn can indicate pregnancy, a nearby initial giving a clue as to who will be so blessed! To another, the same symbol near the rim of the cup can foretell financial success; halfway down it is equated with good health; and at the bottom it suggests that both health and finances are due for a boost. A third reader may see the acorn as a general sign of health and plenty. It is useful to learn the basic meanings of the symbols, then as you gain experience you will learn to form your own ideas about the meaning of each one.

Acorn See above.

Aircraft An unexpected journey that may be linked with a disappointment. It may also mean new projects and an increase in status.

Anchor A journey will come to a successful end. If the querent is currently having a bumpy ride through life, stability will soon be restored. An anchor at the top of the cup can indicate a boost in business; in the middle it means a voyage that boosts prosperity; near the bottom it suggests that social success is beckoning.

Angel Heralds good news or indicates protection.

Ant Industry and hard work lie ahead, perhaps working with others to bring a project to a happy completion.

Apple Achievement and a rosy future in business; as apples are symbols of fertility, they also represent good health.

Arch Links the querent with marriage or long-term relationships. Someone regarded as an enemy may be about to extend the hand of friendship.

Arrow Usually means bad news. If the arrow points towards the querent, he or she may be in danger of an attack of some kind; if it points away, the querent may be the one on the offensive. However, there is a school of thought that sees arrows as bearers of good news in career and financial matters.

Axe The questioner may have to chop away unpleasant difficulties.

Baby Presages the birth of a child or can indicate new interests and creative projects. Babies can sometimes indicate small worries.

Bag Warning that a trap may be about to ensnare the querent.

Baggage A holiday or trip away from home. It can also signify that the questioner is carrying about unnecessary emotional baggage which should be dumped as soon as possible.

Ball Indicates that the querent will soon be bouncing back from current difficulties and that a situation can be changed. A ball can also suggest that someone involved in sport will have a significant influence in the matter.

Ball and chain Current responsibilities are weighing heavily on the querent and need to be released.

Balloon Suggests that troubles may float into one's life, but they will soon drift off again.

Basket A sign that can carry gifts with it. If the basket is full, someone close to the querent could have news of a pregnancy. An empty basket can mean that the questioner is giving too much of himself or herself to others.

Bear Travel to a foreign land is on the cards. A bear can also signify that a strong ally will offer protection in a time of need and that he or she will give you the strength to resolve a difficult situation.

Bee Change of some sort is in store for family or close friends.

Bell Marriage is in the air.

Bird Good news may soon be winging its way into the querent's life. If the bird is flying away from the handle, a departure could be round the corner, perhaps a fledgling is about to leave the nest. If the bird is flying towards the handle, a new opportunity is on the way.

Boat An important discovery is on the horizon. A boat also signifies a visit from a friend and indicates that soon a safe harbour will be reached.

Book If open, a book suggests good news. A closed book means that a delay of some sort will affect plans for the future and a secret must be uncovered.

Boot Indicates achievement. If the querent is seeking protection for some reason, it will be theirs. However, if the boot is pointing away from the handle, then a dismissal of some sort is likely.

Bottle A full bottle is a sign encouraging the querent to channel energy into a new challenge. An empty bottle is a sign of exhaustion and suggests health matters may soon be a cause for concern.

Box When open, a box suggests that any romantic problems afflicting the questioner will soon vanish. When closed, it can mean that something hidden will present itself.

Bracelet A friendship or marriage partnership.

Branch If in leaf, branches herald birth or regeneration. If bare, then a disappointment of some sort is indicated.

Bridge An opportunity for success will soon cross the querent's path.

Broom Suggests that a good clear-out (physically and emotionally) is needed.

Building A change of address may be just around the corner.

Bull Suggests force, stubbornness and fighting will ensue.

Butterfly Innocent pleasures are about to flutter through the questioner's life, offering regeneration and encouraging a carefree attitude. The symbol can also suggest frivolity and fickleness.

Cage A sign that something is holding the questioner back. However, a cage is also a sign of encouragement as it indicates the shackles will soon be shrugged off and it will be time to move ahead again. A cage sometimes indicates a marriage proposal!

Candle Hidden matters will come to light and new ideas will form.

Cannon Can indicate a battle or conquest. *See* Gun.

Castle Suggests circumstances are about to improve, perhaps through a marriage union. A strong character and success are indicated.

Cat Suggests treachery when appearing in the tea leaves and may represent a false friend.

Chain Links with other people will strengthen. Can indicate a marriage proposal or wedding.

Chair Indicates a guest will pay a visit.

Cherry Indicates a love affair.

Chess piece A short-tem project should be put to one side. It it is time to plan for the long term if looming troubles are to be overcome. The symbol also suggests that people are manoeuvring themselves into position for an oncoming conflict and it is time for the querent to do the same.

Cliff The querent may be about to walk into a dangerous situation. However, a cliff can also suggest the time has come to cast convention aside and live a little dangerously.

Cloud Indicates doubts, but they should soon clear.

Clover A lucky symbol, heralding prosperity.

Coffin Signifies a loss of some kind.

Coin Money and good fortune are on the way. Debts will be repaid. A coin may also represent something valuable to the querent.

Cow Prosperity and tranquil times are ahead. Enjoy them while they last – the herd may soon move on to pastures new.

Cross Can suggest sacrifice and suffering or protection in a matter.

Crown Honours are about to be bestowed on the querent; a dream may come true.

Cup Indicates love, emotional fulfillment and abundance.

Daffodil A welcome harbinger, not only of spring and a fresh start, but also of wealth and happiness just around the corner.

Dagger Warns of danger, especially if impetuous actions are taken. A sudden shock could be in store, brought about by the plotting of enemies.

Daisy Happiness and simple pleasures are indicated.

Devil Bad influences are at work. No good can come from pursuing a particular path.

Dice Taking a risk may result in fortune.

Dog Good friends are on the way, especially if the dog is running towards the handle.

Donkey Patience and hard work are needed.

Door An opportunity is being offered. If the door is open, a step into the unknown can be taken with confidence. If the door is closed, the opportunity is not yet available and patience is required.

Dots As well as indicating money-making opportunities, dots also accentuate the meaning of any nearby symbol.

Dove Good fortune is on its way.

Dragon A warning of danger; unforeseen troubles may be on their way.

Drum Quarrels and disagreements, scandal and gossip are indicated. Drums can also herald a call to action.

Duck Brings the chance to travel by water and suggests opportunities from abroad. Ducks can also indicate wealth and suggest that we will soon find our true vocation.

Ear The questioner should be attentive, for important news is on its way.

Egg Signifies fertility, pregnancy and the development of a new creative project.

Eggtimer If the querent is faced with completing a task of some sort, time may be running out.

Elephant Signifies wisdom and lasting success; can represent a trustworthy friend.

Envelope Brings good news of some kind.

Eye When eyes are seen in the cup they warn us to proceed with caution and keep a careful watch over matters.

Face When the face is smiling it is a sign of happiness and success, but if frowning it suggests that obstacles will stand in the way of a matter. Several faces suggest a gathering or imply that many people have influence over a matter.

Fairy Indicates joy and wishes fulfilled.

Fan Suggests a flirtation, perhaps leading to some sort of indiscretion.

Feather A sign that indiscretion and instability will upset the questioner in some way.

Feet An important decision will have to be made in the near future and the querent will need to act quickly to ensure success. Travel may be necessary.

Fence A warning that limitations are about to be imposed that will restrict the querent's options, perhaps because someone is being overprotective.

Finger When pointing to another sign, a finger emphasises the other sign's meaning.

Fingernail Points to unfair accusations being made.

Fish Good fortune, often the result of lucky speculation. Fish may also indicate that foreign travel is on the horizon.

Flag Brings a warning of danger. To overcome it, the querent will need to rally resources and act courageously.

Flies Indicate minor irritations.

Flowers Either a single flower or a bunch presages a celebration of some sort. Flowers also signify the questioner will be showered with small kindnesses that will bring great happiness. A single stem can mean love is about to appear. If the flowers take the form of a garland, then recognition and promotion lie ahead.

Fork A warning to beware of false flattery and untrustworthy friends.

Fountain Success lies in store for the querent. Fountains also indicate sexual passion.

Fox Signifies cunning and manipulation. Aims can be achieved by using persuasion, but not at the expense of honesty.

Frog Suggests that the questioner has the happy knack of fitting in, no matter where he or she is. Frogs can also presage some sort of change, perhaps of address.

Fruit A sign of prosperous times ahead. *See also* Apple, Cherry, Grapes.

Gallows Some kind of loss is about to occur – it might be a financial loss or it could be a friendship. Gallows can also indicate that the querent is feeling trapped in a potentially dangerous situation. Conversely, if the questioner is not in the best of health, gallows are a sign of an improvement.

Gate When open, gates signify that great prosperity and happiness are in store. When closed, they warn not to proceed with a plan and suggest obstacles lie ahead.

Geese A signal to heed warnings that are given – ignore them at your peril!

Giant A person with a magnetic and dominant personality is involved in a matter. Giants also herald that huge strides will be made in the querent's career.

Glove Indicates a challenge.

Goat Warns of possible enemies.

Grapes Presage prosperity, a sign that we should squeeze every drop of opportunity from chances that are about to present themselves. Grapes are a sign of good health. They suggest this is a time to indulge yourself. It could also be a period during which your dreams come true.

Grass Suggests an inner restlessness and warns that a matter is about to cause discontent.

Guitar Harmonious meetings, perhaps leading to romance.

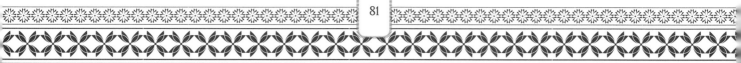

Gun Anger and revenge. Guns are also a warning that, unless properly channelled, an outburst of aggression may have unfortunate results.

Hammock Associated with relaxation, hammocks suggest an unconventional nature and perhaps a desire to opt out of responsibilities and take things easy.

Hands When open and outstretched, hands foretell that a new friendship is about to be forged. If they are closed, an argument is indicated and someone may act in a very mean way which is quite out of character.

Hat A signal that change is the air, perhaps in the shape of a new job. Headgear may also herald the arrival of an unexpected visitor or an invitation to a formal occasion.

Hawk Jealousy may be indicated. Rivals are watching for signs of weakness and getting ready to pounce.

Head Be on the lookout for new opportunities that could result in a promotion to a new position of authority.

Heart Indicates a romance that will lead to a long-term relationship and perhaps marriage. Can also represent another close bond or relationship.

Hen Can indicate a happy home life. It may also foretell that an older person, probably a maternal type, will come to have an increasing influence in the querent's life.

Hill A warning that the path ahead may be full of ups and downs, but the problems will be overcome easily. Once the troubles are behind you, long-term ambitions will be achieved.

Horn A welcome sign that will bring an abundance of happiness and peace.

Horse Brings good news, possibly from a lover. If the horse is at full stretch, galloping across the cup, it indicates that the time may have come to saddle up and get travelling. If the horse is harnessed to a cart, a change of job or address is beckoning – this is very advantageous if the cart is full.

Horseshoe Heralds good luck.

Hourglass Suggests that a decision needs to be made quickly and that the querent is running out of time.

House A matter is secure and there is nothing to fear. Domestic matters are highlighted.

Iceberg Warns of approaching danger. The matter in question has hidden depths; if they are not recognised, there could be trouble in store.

Igloo Indicates temporary refuge from an emotional situation that is causing problems.

Initials Represent the people whose names begin with the initials; any nearby symbols refer to these people rather than the querent.

Ink A squirt of ink represent doubts that must be clarified before the querent signs an important document, probably a legal one.

Inkpot Indicates that there are important legal or official matters to be communicated in writing.

Insect Suggests little problems will arise.

Islands A holiday, perhaps to an exotic location, is coming up. Can also indicate that the querent is feeling increasingly isolated in a matter.

Jewels Indicate that someone is about to bestow an unexpected gift of a very generous nature on the querent.

Jug A full jug indicates happiness, abundance and good health. An empty jug is a warning that fortunes are being frittered away.

Kettle Suggests domestic happiness, particularly when near the handle. However, if it is near the bottom of the cup it indicates problems in the domestic realm.

Key A sign of new opportunities. Two keys at the bottom of the cup warn of a burglary. They can also signify increasing independence, perhaps of a child about to fly the nest.

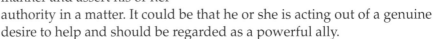

King Can warn that an older person will act in a high-handed manner and assert his or her authority in a matter. It could be that he or she is acting out of a genuine desire to help and should be regarded as a powerful ally.

Kite Wishes will come true and aspirations will be successfully achieved.

Knife Warns that a relationship is about to come to an end – the nearer the knife is to the top of the cup, the sooner that end will be. At the very top, then divorce is in the air.

Ladder Presages that the querent will advance in a particular area. It could mean promotion at work or it could be in another matter. A ladder is also a sign that this is the time to set sights high and achieve your greatest ambitions.

Leaves A welcome sign that good fortune is about to smile on us, bringing prosperity. Falling leaves foretell that some sort of natural turning point will be reached that will bring a surge of happiness; this may occur by the autumn.

Letter Brings news from afar.

Line Straight lines indicate progress, perhaps a journey. Slanting lines speak of failure in business. Curved lines herald disappointment and uncertainty on the horizon.

Lion As the king of the jungle, he signifies powerful friends.

Lizard A sign to get in touch with primitive instincts and to trust them. Also a warning to check facts carefully, as the source may not be as reliable as it seems.

Loop Indicates that the path ahead is a circuitous one and we may feel as though we are going round in circles and getting nowhere.

Magnet We will be drawn to new interests, perhaps a relationship will blossom out of an attraction.

Man Can indicate a particular man or a visitor. If the arms are outstretched, then the man will come bearing gifts.

Map May suggest travel or signify that after a long period of uncertainty life will get back on track.

Maypole New life is stirring after a period of dormancy. May also herald news of a pregnancy or that a project started in the spring will come to a happy conclusion.

Mermaid Passion will lead to temptation and temptation to infidelity and infidelity to heartbreak.

Mirror Might indicate that the querent has a vain nature or that he or she feels that life is passing them by. A situation is forcing the querent to face some truths about himself or herself.

Mole Suggests that secrets are in the air and, when revealed, they will have a significant effect on the questioner's life. A mole may indicate a false friend who may be doing something to undermine the querent.

Monk See Nun.

Moon One of the most frequently seen symbols in the cup. A full moon signifies that a love affair is in the offing, a waxing moon suggests new projects will prosper and a waning moon warns of a decline in fortune. If the moon is partially obscured, then depression is suggested. If it is surrounded by little dots, then a prosperous union is in the air.

Mountain Can be a sign that obstacles, more serious ones than those indicated by hills, will appear and block the querent's path. Mountains also stand for high ambitions that may or may not be achieved.

Mouse Signifies oncoming poverty, perhaps as the result of theft. A mouse may also indicate that this is not the time to be timid and, if initiative is taken now, the benefits will be substantial.

Nail Suggests malice, pain and injustice. The querent will have to fight hard.

Necklace Suggests a secret admirer who, when he presents himself, may turn out to be the querent's partner through life. A broken necklace warns of a friendship that may be about to end.

Needle Needles imply admiration and can suggest that the best way to deal with jealous criticism is to brush it aside.

Nest Signifies that domestic matters are about to come to the fore; highlights the need to settle down with a family of one's own.

Net The questioner is feeling trapped by or worried about a new venture. Something that has long been held back is about to present itself.

Numbers Refer to the symbol they are closest to in the teacup and may indicate the number of days that will elapse before that particular event takes place. The number may also be taken to have its own meaning, as follows:

1 represents creativity, energy and new beginnings
2 is a sign of duality and rivalry, while at the same time possibly promising a betrothal
3 represents harmony
4 suggests that now is the time to accept limits and work within them
5 signifies that clear communication is needed when dealing with others
6 is a sign of peaceful and harmonious times
7 points towards the unconscious world and suggests it is time to put things into long-term perspective
8 cautions the querent to follow convention
9 suggests self-interest; it also signifies a satisfactorily completed project

Nun Indicates a desire to go into retreat and withdraw from life for a while to ponder the best way forward. Monks and nuns may also represent wise friends who are willing to help whenever called upon.

Oars Suggest the time has come to stop waiting for others to help and to find a solution yourself, perhaps by travelling to a new location.

Octopus Danger is about to entwine the querent in its tentacles, probably because he or she has taken on too much either in business or in his or her personal life. An octopus can also represent a talent for multi-tasking!

Ostrich Well known for burying its head in the sand when danger threatens, this suggests that the querent will be inclined to do the same.

Owl Warns of trouble ahead, possibly brought about by gossip and scandal, or perhaps by a failure of some sort. An owl warns of neglected tasks, but can also signify that a very wise person is standing by to help.

Oyster Indicates that the querent has hidden depths and talents which, if uncovered and used at the right time, will be of tremendous benefit.

Padlock When open, suggests a pleasant opportunity is on its way. When closed, a warning that we should hold back and avoid forcing a matter.

Palm tree Success will bring honour to the querent. With its exotic associations, the tree may be a sign that travel to a foreign location is on the cards.

Parachute The querent will escape from danger; help is on the way.

Parallel lines Suggest the smooth passage of plans.

Parrot A warning that passing on gossip could be dangerous. Foreign travel may also be indicated.

Path A new path will appear in the questioner's life. If straight, then the way ahead will be smooth. A fork in the path suggests that a choice will have to be made – the wider the fork, the more important the choice.

Peacock Represents wealth, riches and a happy marriage union.

Pendulum Suggests that time is running out.

Pig Greed, indulgence or material success.

Pigeon Important news will be received.

Pipe Careful thought needs to be given to a problem. The querent should keep an open mind.

Pistol Warns of danger and that someone will use unpleasant methods to get their own way.

Purse Presages luck or gain.

Pyramid Represents lasting wealth and honour. *See also* Triangle.

Question mark Hesitancy and caution are advisable.

Rabbit Represents fertility. Also indicates the need to move swiftly in a matter.

Rainbow Signifies that wishes are about to be fulfilled.

Rat Warns of treacherous individuals.

Raven Bad news and disappointment of some kind.

Ring If close to the rim of the cup, a ring can indicate marriage. If near the middle, a proposal can soon be expected. If at the bottom, the engagement will be a long one. If the ring is complete, the marriage will be happy. If the ring is incomplete, the engagement will be broken off.

Road See Path.

Rocks Signify obstacles and hazards along life's pathway. These should be small enough to be overcome and, with a little careful planning, can be used as building bricks or stepping stones to a better future.

Rose Love, happiness and fortune.

Scale Judgement and justice. Balanced scales represent a just, fair decision that will bring benefits; unbalanced scales suggest that the querent will suffer injustice.

Scissors Presage domestic arguments that can result in separation.

Seesaw Suggests a situation is changeable; mood swings are indicated.

Shark Signifies attack from an unexpected source.

Shell Represents good news and discoveries of an emotional nature.

Ship Journeys across water will be beneficial to the querent.

Snake Traditionally a symbol of treachery, betrayal and misfortune. May represent an enemy. Snakes also suggest it is time for the querent to shed old, outdated habits and start afresh.

Spider Signifies that money will come to the querent. Can also suggest that someone may be spinning a web of deceit to ensnare the querent.

Spinning wheel Careful planning and consistent industry will bring good results, but this sign also warns that someone may be plotting against the querent from behind the scenes.

Square Once seen as a sign of restriction, but now generally taken to mean stability and protection. If the querent works hard to fulfil his responsibilities, financial and material rewards are promised.

Squirrel Signifies that rewards will be reaped after a period of hard work and frugality.

Star A five-pointed star indicates that health, hope and happiness await.

Sun Happiness and success will shine down on the querent. Self-confidence and empowerment are indicated. The summer will be a happy one.

Swan Good fortune and a long-term romance.

Sword Suggests the querent should be prepared for quarrels and disputes.

Table Indicates a social occasion.

Teapot Represents a meeting.

Tent Represents travel and an unsettled life.

Telescope Represents adventure into the unknown. The answers to present mysteries will soon be revealed.

Tortoise Associated with longevity, protection and a love of tradition. Goals are achieved slowly but surely.

Tower Can imply restrictions. However, if the tower has steps it may lead to a rise in status and a boost in finances. An incomplete tower suggests that plans are not yet finished.

Train Journeys and visitors are indicated.

Tree Prosperity, brought about by long-held ambitions.

Triangle Indicates unexpected success if pointing upwards or unexpected failure if pointing downwards. Opportunities are available; it is up to the querent to grab them.

Tunnel Present confusion and setbacks will soon be resolved.

Umbrella Suggests that the querent is about to be showered with minor problems. If the umbrella is open, then the querent will have protection; if the umbrella is closed, then the querent will not be adequately prepared to weather the storm.

Unicorn Brings promise of magical insights that illuminate the querent's life in some way; also indicates that an unusual and unexpected opportunity is on the horizon.

Urn Happiness and prosperity.

Violin *See* Guitar.

Volcano Presages an eruption of passionate emotion. Volcanoes may appear when the querent is seething with anger, but determined not to let it show.

Walking stick Heralds the arrival of a visitor.

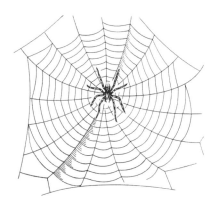

Waterfall Represents a shower of good fortune and prosperity.

Wasp Signifies anger and romantic quarrels.

Weathervane Points to inconsistent and unreliable friends.

Web *See* Spider.

Whale Indicates professional success and prosperity.

Wheel If the wheel is complete, it represents good fortune; if the wheel is broken, then disappointment looms.

Windmill Hard work will bring success.

Window Represents good luck if open, and bad luck if shut. A window may offer new insights or a chance to explore new horizons, but a curtained window means that other people's narrow horizons are holding the querent back.

Wolf Harmful jealousy and possessiveness.

Woman May represent a particular woman the querent knows or is about to meet.

Yacht Wealth and happiness.

Zebra An exciting adventure abroad.

CRYSTAL GAZING

WHEN WE THINK OF DIVINATION, one of the caricatures that comes to mind is an old crone peering into a crystal ball. This image is often used to ridicule divinatory practices. However, crystal gazing, along with other forms of scrying, has a long and honourable tradition.

Crystal gazing is a form of scrying, a method of divination that involves peering at a shiny, translucent or luminescent surface such as a crystal, a mirror or a flickering flame. The seer enters a trance-like state where images appear on the surface of the object or in the mind's eye. From these images, the seer can assess a particular situation from a wider perspective and foretell the outcome if the querent continues along his or her current path.

As with all methods of divination, crystal gazing is used to develop wisdom and self-knowledge as well as to peer into the future to see what fortunes await us. The seer can help the querent make the right choices to bring about the most positive outcome in a matter as well as address what other unseen influences might be at work.

THE HISTORY OF CRYSTAL GAZING

Crystal gazing is one of many methods of divination which have their roots in prehistory, and from which related practices have developed in different parts of the world. Some of the earliest accounts of scrying date from ancient Egypt and Greece. Scrying is also believed to have been practised by the Celts, the Native Americans and others. It was extremely popular in medieval Europe, as were most of the other forms of divination that we continue to use today.

One of the most famous scryers in history was Michele de Nostradame, known as Nostradamus, the famous sixteenth-century doctor, astrologer and seer from Saint Rémy de Provence in France, whose prophecies continue to unfold many centuries after his death. He is believed to have used a bowl of water held in a brass tripod to gaze into the future. From these visions he made his prophecies which were set out in his famous book of quatrains, the *Centuries*, in 1555. The prophecies were written in a cryptic form, difficult to decipher; Nostradamus claimed that this was to avoid persecution by the Spanish Inquisition.

Around the same time in England, Dr John Dee, mathematician, astronomer, astrologer and, famously, consultant to Queen Elizabeth I, was using crystal balls and various methods of scrying in his work.

In folklore there are celebration days upon which young girls are likely to see the face of their future husband in a mirror (Hallowe'en) or in a bowl

NOSTRADAMUS

of water (Midsummer's Day). These traditions have grown out of age-old divinatory practices used to answer questions about love and marriage prospects, together with other questions about our lives and what the future may hold.

SELECTING YOUR CRYSTAL BALL

Traditionally the ball used for crystal gazing should be a gift from a person with the talent, but today crystal balls are readily available from specialist crystal shops, exhibitions or online. Although usually made from clear quartz crystal, there are many different types to choose from. You can also use a glass ball, which is significantly cheaper than crystal, but lacks the powerful properties of the genuine article.

Each crystal has particular qualities and magical uses. Generally red, yellow, orange and brown (hot-coloured) stones have creative energy and their meaning is active. Green, blue, purple, pink and pearly white stones encourage emotional and spiritual wellbeing and harmony and describe more passive qualities. Black and other darker stones represent depth and intensity and are usually not recommended for newcomers to the art.

The associations of some of the more commonly used crystals are as follows:

Agate	Strength, protection, security, wellbeing
Amethyst	Spirituality, psychic ability, healing, the imagination
Aventurine	Opportunity, expansion, adventure
Beryl	Balance, healing, relaxation, intuition
Carnelian	Energy, confidence, passion
Citrine	Joy, hope, health, wellbeing
Emerald	Fertility, love, hope
Jade	Luck, health, wisdom, protection

Red jasper	Vitality, courage, protection
Lapis lazuli	Mental clarity, balance, inspiration
Obsidian	Depth, power, protection, grounding
Clear quartz	Purifying, healing, awakening, mental clarity
Rose quartz	Love, romance, matters of the heart, healing, forgiveness
Smoky quartz	Healing, mental clarity, balance
Ruby	Love, passion, power, confidence
Sapphire	Loyalty, truth, psychic ability
Tiger's eye	Strength, courage, grounding
Unakite	Rest, relaxation, composure

As with any form of divination, preferences vary from person to person. In general the ball should be as clear as possible and free from any distracting blemishes or bubbles. However, some people find these features help to concentrate their gaze and open the doorway to the imagination and the psychic realm.

When searching for a crystal ball that is right for you, ensure you are in a relaxed and receptive state of mind. If you are in a shop, look around and try handling the crystal balls that appeal to you. Consider how they make you feel. Does your eye keep returning to one or does one stand out as right for you? If not, then you may need to keep searching.

PREPARING YOUR CRYSTAL BALL

To prepare the crystal ball, wash it in water, then polish it with a soft cloth. Some gazers place their crystal by a window during a full moon and use the moon's light to cleanse the stone and remove any residual energies of previous gazers. This practice may be repeated once a month or as required. When it is not in use, the ball should be kept out of general view, perhaps wrapped in a cloth or pouch, and should not be handled by anyone other than the user.

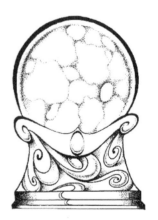

ARRANGING THE ROOM FOR THE READING

Many seers find a dimly lit room is best – some people use candlelight to achieve this, others swathe lamps with suitable (flame-resistant) cloths. The room should be quiet and free from disturbance. Time each session with a watch or clock positioned so that you can see its face, but make

sure you are not distracted by its ticking. The first occasion should last no longer than ten minutes. Gradually increase the time of each session, up to around twenty minutes maximum.

The crystal ball should be placed on a black cloth on a table. The seer should sit facing the ball.

To begin with it is best to conduct the sessions alone, as the presence of another person can be distracting. As you gain experience, you will be able to answer people's questions and allow them to be present during the reading. If reading for another person, you can seat the querent nearby. He or she should remain quiet and still throughout the reading, unless the gazer indicates otherwise.

HOW TO GAZE INTO THE BALL

Step 1: Relax and clear your mind. Some people can achieve this by deep breathing, others use visualisation techniques.

Step 2: Hold the crystal in your hands for a few moments to get attuned to it. While doing this, decide on the purpose of the reading and clarify the question in your mind without pondering it too deeply.

Step 3: Now return the crystal to its stand and gently fix your gaze at the light reflecting off it. Gradually your vision will go out of focus and 'misty' and images will appear. The images may appear in the ball or in your mind's eye. They should not be forced but allowed to occur naturally. You should let them come and go freely without trying to control them.

Step 4: You may want to write down what you see as it occurs. You can interpret it later.

Learning to scry is a talent that takes time to develop. Some people see images from the first time they try it, but others have to keep practising before any images appear, so you may need to be persistent if you want to master this form of divination. Learning to scry can improve your concentration and help develop your intuition and psychic abilities, so the rewards of perseverance are well worth the effort.

INTERPRETING WHAT YOU SEE

Once the images appear, you need to interpret their meaning. Often the answer will appear in symbols, as it does in many other methods of divination. The symbols might take the form of colours, shapes, people, animals, objects or moving images; they may be woven into a narrative, as though you are viewing a film or play. In each case the gazer needs to learn the meanings of the symbols before the images can be understood.

Symbols are generally interpreted in the same way across the different divinatory systems, although their meanings vary from culture to culture and from one historical period to another. Current cultural references are added to traditional meanings because scrying is a living system that gains new associations (and sheds older ones) over time. In addition, each of us has personal associations based on our life experiences and these should be incorporated into our interpretation of what we see.

Colours

Colours have symbolic significance in scrying. The following meanings can be used as a general guideline, but you may want to develop your own associations with each of these colours to personalise what you see:

White   Purity, clarity, temperance, safety, protection, kindness, good fortune, fresh start

Yellow   Joy, vitality, creativity, money, success, confidence, communication, conscious realm

Orange   Energy, excitement, stimulation, appetite, optimism, possible stress or turbulence

Pink   Love, romance, friendship, happiness, lightheartedness, matters of the heart

Red   Energy, enthusiasm, action, heat, passion, sexuality, adventure, endurance, possible danger or aggression

Purple   Spirituality, intuition, mystery, imagination, creativity, peace, healing, possible loss of boundaries

Blue   Peace, calm, clarity, truth, beauty, tranquillity, coolness, orderliness, high ideals

Green   Growth, creativity, health, fertility, nature, renewal, regeneration, harmony, relaxation

Brown   Groundedness, stability, authority, responsibility, tradition, institution, achievement, fertility

| Grey | Wisdom, maturity, cooperation, neutrality, knowledge, possible sadness or mourning |
| Black | Shadows, secrets, hidden places, peace, unconscious realm, possible misfortune |

Symbols

Images that are scried sometimes take the form of shapes, people, animals, objects and symbols. Their meanings can be interpreted in a similar way to that of tea-leaf reading (see pages 68–91).

Objects appearing in the background lie further into the future than objects appearing in the foreground of the vision.

Moving images

If the gazer sees moving images with a coherent story, it could be that the answer is straightforward and self-explanatory and there is no need to interpret symbols. For example, the question may be – will a relationship result in marriage? If the crystal ball reveals a wedding celebration for the two individuals concerned, it may simply affirm that the marriage will take place.

However, the images may tell a story that has no direct connection with the question itself. In this case, it is useful for the gazer to view it in a more symbolic way, as with dreams, in order to discover the message of the reading. For example, if the question is again about marriage and the gazer sees a king locking a princess in a tower, this may suggest that an authority figure with great power, possibly the girl's father, will object to the marriage and try to prevent the lovers being together. A similar meaning may be conveyed by a more obscure image of a pink flower (love) being crushed by a lion (the king or father), or even a dove (love and the marriage union) being locked away (obstacle) in a brown (authority) box.

OTHER METHODS OF CRYSTAL DIVINATION

Crystal ball reading is not the only method of crystal and gemstone divination. There are hundreds of gemstones and crystals, each with its own qualities and meanings. You might want to keep an assortment of crystals and gemstones in a pouch. While focusing on a question, you can take out the first stone your fingers touch and glean an answer from it according to the list given earlier in this chapter.

I CHING

THE BOOK OF CHANGES

THE I CHING is a system of divination based on hexagrams. A hexagram is a combination of six horizontal lines – there are 64 hexagrams in the I Ching, each one symbolising particular qualities. The diviner casts a hexagram and uses it to answer questions about the future and to gain further insight into matters.

This system of divination developed alongside the Taoist philosophy of Ancient China and is based on the principles of *yin* and *yang*, the balance of opposites and the changing nature of the universe. The name 'I Ching' translates as 'The Book of Changes'.

ORIGINS OF THE I CHING

The I Ching appears in some of the oldest texts in China; its current format dates from around the fifth century BCE. The use of symbolic hexagrams may have developed from the practice of divining with turtle and tortoise shells or animal bones, as the lines of the cracks in the shells and bones are similar to the lines we find in the I Ching.

There are many myths about the origin of the I Ching. According to one story, the Chinese Emperor Fu Hsi (circa. 2800 BCE) was meditating by a river when suddenly a dragon-like creature rose from the water. Fu Hsi, curious rather than scared, noticed that there were lines on the creature's scales. Intrigued, he contemplated these lines and after a while started to feel that they had made him a wiser man. Wanting to share his discovery so that others might benefit, he set about recording the lines he saw on the scales of the creature. The system he devised took the form of diagrams, consisting of broken and unbroken lines.

It is believed that, later, King Wen of Zhou (1099–1050 BCE) and his son the Duke of Chou defined and developed the system further. The legendary philosopher Confucius is credited with the authorship of a series of commentaries on the hexagrams, known as the 'Ten Wings'.

One of the most enduringly popular translations and commentaries on the I Ching, which has served to introduce the system to the West over the last century, is *The I Ching* or *Book of Changes* by Richard Wilhelm. Many of the meanings we use are based on this translation.

THE STRUCTURE OF THE HEXAGRAM

There are two different types of line that make up each six-line hexagram of the I Ching:

The solid, unbroken lines represent the masculine and active *yang* principle which governs Heaven.

The broken lines represent the feminine and passive *yin* principle which governs the Earth.

These lines are grouped into sets of three, known as trigrams. There are eight possible combinations of these trigrams. Each trigram symbolises a different aspect of Heaven, Earth and humanity.

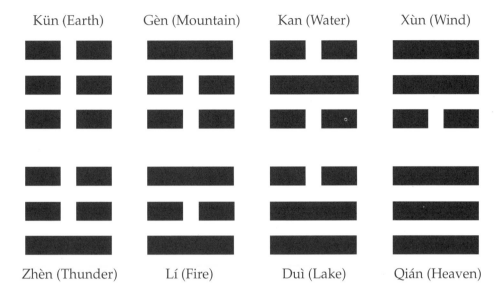

Kün (Earth)   Gèn (Mountain)   Kan (Water)   Xùn (Wind)

Zhèn (Thunder)   Lí (Fire)   Duì (Lake)   Qián (Heaven)

HOW TO CAST A HEXAGRAM

Once the question to be answered has been carefully framed in the mind of the querent, the hexagram can be cast. The traditional method of casting involves the use of fifty yarrow stalks that are divided and counted using an elaborate set of procedures. Given the complexity of this method, it was inevitable that a simpler system would develop and today the most popular way of casting a hexagram is to use three identical coins.

Various other methods are used, some involving dice or beads. There are also numerous internet sites and computer programmes that will select the trigrams for you using the same odds as the yarrow stalk method.

Three-coin method

To use the standard coin method, you will need three identical coins. Traditional Chinese coins can be bought specially for this purpose if preferred, although any coin can be used. When using modern coins, the 'tails' side is usually taken to represent *yin* and the 'heads' side to represent *yang*.

The coins are thrown down together a total of six times. Each throw determines one line of the hexagram. The first throw gives the bottom line, the second throw gives the next line up and so on, until the sixth throw, which gives the top line. In this way, a six-line hexagram is created. A value of three is assigned to each 'head' and a value of two is assigned to each 'tail'. You should add up the value of the three coins in each throw and write it down.

For example, a head (3) plus two tails (2 + 2) gives a total of 7 (3 + 2 + 2 = 7).

Each total can only amount to 6, 7, 8 or 9.

Number	Meaning	Symbol
6	Old *yin* (*yin* changing into *yang*)	—X—
7	Young *yang* (unchanging *yang*)	———
8	Young *yin* (unchanging *yin*)	—— ——
9	Old *yang* (*yang* changing into *yin*)	—O—

Depending on the number, each line has the quality of changing (old) or unchanging (young). Old is considered to be more powerful than young.

Initially, the changing lines are read as if they were ordinary *yin* and *yang* lines. This is the primary hexagram, which represents the present time. Once the primary hexagram has been created and the meaning explored, the lines are reversed – a changing *yin* line becomes an unbroken *yang* line, and a changing *yang* line becomes a broken *yin* line. The meaning of the changing hexagram indicates the future and the direction in which things are moving.

SAMPLE READING

For example, the querent asks the general question 'How can I progress in my career?' The coins are thrown and two hexagrams are created, as described at the top of the opposite page.

Throw	Total	Symbol	Primary Hexagram	Changing/ Unchanging	Changing Hexagram
Sixth	6	—X—	—— ——	Changing	————
Fifth	6	—X—	—— ——	Changing	————
Fourth	6	—X—	————	Changing	————
Third	9	—O—	————	Changing	—— ——
Second	8	—— ——	—— ——	Unchanging	—— ——
First	7	————	————	Unchanging	————

The Present

The primary hexagram in this example is:

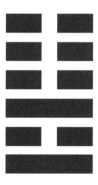

Hexagram 36: Míng Yí – Darkening of the Light

This hexagram suggests that at present the querent should not worry about finding a new job or changing career because he or she could get bogged down in making too many plans. The querent should concentrate on fulfilling plans which he or she has already made and not be concerned if things are going badly – they will soon get better.

The future

The changing hexagram in this example is:

Hexagram 25: Wú Wàng – Correctness

This hexagram indicates that the querent will need to respect the limits of his or her situation and not endeavour to go beyond them at the moment. Selflessness and simplicity are the key to success. Any problems will be temporary and it is important to prepare for the time when they will have lifted.

SUMMARY OF MEANINGS

1. Qián – The Creative

Success is assured through the questioner's strength, power and persistence. Plans can be continued with confidence, as long as there is no over-reaching or overstretching of resources.

2. Kūn – The Receptive

The future can be viewed with confidence as things will come to pass, but in their own time. As success may lie in other people's hands, the questioner is advised to be still, responsive and receptive to advice.

3. Zhèn – Initial Difficulty

Opportunities that present themselves should be viewed with care as they might spell danger. If help is needed, don't be afraid to ask for it. Proceed with caution – there is no need to act hastily.

4. Méng – Innocence

There may be a lack of experience or even wisdom in a matter, so listen to the advice of more experienced people and learn from it. Remain enthusiastic and don't give up whatever you do.

5. Xū – Waiting

Patience is a virtue – after all if you plant seeds in a cornfield, you don't expect to harvest the crop straightaway. Help will be at hand when the time is right. Don't force the pace or worry too much. Wait and be ready.

6. Sòng – Conflict

There is a need to resolve conflicts. Impulsive action, arguments and aggressive behaviour are to be avoided. If criticism is offered, accept and learn from it. Listen to advice and things will improve.

7. Shī – The Army

Trust is the key to true leadership. Remaining honest and fair will help gain the respect of those who work for you. Discipline and integrity should be incorporated into everything you do.

 ### 8. Bǐ – Union

This is the time to build strong bonds by sharing experiences with others. Help them and you will find that you are helping yourself at the same time. Bǐ is an indication of harmonious partnerships.

 ### 9. Xiǎo Chù – Taming Force

Now is the time to use your strength and power to clear small obstacles from your path so that you are ready for the future. Although times may be hard, be grateful for small mercies. Restraint may be called for.

 ### 10. Lǚ – Treading Carefully

Stick to the path you have chosen and press forward without hesitating.

 ### 11. Tài – Tranquillity

Good fortune and harmony are all around; enjoy and share them with others. This is a good time for planning for the future and for steady progress, but beware of the temptation to act rashly.

 ### 12. Pǐ – Stagnation

This is not the time to force the pace, even if you are sure that there are rewards to be had. Modesty is called for if the change in the air is to be turned to your advantage.

 ### 13. Tóng Rén – Companionship

There are benefits to working with others as long as everyone sticks to their allocated tasks. This is a time for sharing. Travel may be indicated.

14. Dà Yǒu – Great Possession

Work hard, lay down for the future and success will be yours.

15. Qiān – Modesty

Arrogance is the enemy of true greatness. Take pride, but in moderation. Be modest and others will give you the help you need. Don't take things at face value – learn to look beneath the surface.

16. Yù – Enthusiasm

Revitalise your spirit through celebration. Give your partner a pleasant surprise. Do not underestimate the power of shared enthusiasm – it will help to increase confidence and limit future difficulties.

17. Suí – Following

Now is the time to take a back seat and leave others in charge. Be as flexible as you can to avoid conflict. Take a relaxed view of things but don't let your goals slip from view.

18. Gǔ – Restoration

Honesty is the best policy, so if you have made mistakes in the past, now is the time to rectify them. Think hard before moving forward and proceed with care.

19. Lín – Approach

Move forward with care and with consideration for the feelings of others. Rash decisions will be especially costly at the moment and may jeopardise your good fortune.

20. Guān – Observing

A good time to plan for the future and look beneath the surface of things. Joint ventures could pay unexpected dividends, especially if you watch, listen and learn.

21. Shì Kè – Biting Through

Be positive about the success that has been achieved and don't let the negativity of others affect you. There may be a legal matter of some kind to sort out, but you can win.

22. Bì – Adorning

Value beauty, but remember it is only skin deep so do not be taken in by appearances. If a business proposition appears to be too good to be true then it probably is. Focus on enhancing your inner beauty.

23. Bō – Stripping Away

This is not the time for action as the odds are not in your favour. There are disruptions ahead and changes in the air. So wait and do what is needed to prepare for the changes ahead.

24. Fù – Returning

Caution, particularly regarding anything new, is advised. It is a time for patience and careful timing. Plan for the future.

25. Wú Wàng – Correctness

Remember that everything has its limits – don't be tempted to go beyond them. Selflessness and simplicity are key at the moment. Remember that problems are temporary. Enjoy life.

26. Dà Chù – Great Accumulating

Wisdom and resources accumulated should be put to work for the benefit of all. Focus on building your inner strength. Don't fear to seek advice.

27. Yí – Nourishment

Take care of what you eat and drink as well as what you say. Choose your thoughts and words wisely in your relationship and remember to be tolerant. Clear your life of things that are not worthwhile.

28. Dà Quò – Great Exceeding

A warning that a situation has gone beyond your control and you may need to withdraw from it for a while. Failing to do so will spell disaster.

29. Kǎn – Gorge

Take care and be on the lookout for pitfalls. Conflict is in the air – proceed with caution. Have faith in yourself and all will be well.

30. Lí – Radiance

Use your radiance and enthusiasm to illuminate the path ahead. Tend your inner fires and keep them burning so that they can be used to your advantage. Be firm and act correctly and success will come.

31. Xián – Feelings

Be receptive to other people's ideas and try to keep feelings of envy at bay. Help others at every opportunity, but do so genuinely and don't try to take advantage of someone else. Cultivate respect and honour.

32. Héng – Persistence

Set your course and stay with it. Stick to traditional methods and avoid any rash behaviour. If others offer advice, listen to it.

33. Dùn – Retreat

There may be trouble ahead, but if you judge the right time to withdraw from a situation and are practical, you will weather the storm.

34. Dà Zhuàng – The Power of the Great

If you say something, be sure you stick to what you promise. This is a time of good fortune and you will find that others feel a powerful attraction to you. If you act wisely, you will benefit from it.

35. Jìn – Advancement

This is a time when honesty is the best policy. If you are considerate of others, you will be rewarded with advancement.

36. Míng Yí – Darkening of the Light

Try not to get bogged down by making too many plans. Keep to the few that you have and don't be concerned if things go badly for a time – they will soon improve.

37. Jiā Rén – Family

Family matters are to the fore and it will probably be necessary to exercise authority, but try to do so with fairness and tolerance.

38. Kuí – Opposition

Try to keep *yin* and *yang* in balance to help resolve conflicts and disruptions. It is a good time to make small changes; remember that mighty oak trees grow from tiny acorns.

39. Jiǎn – Limping

There are hard times ahead, with problems on the horizon. The only way to solve them is to face them firmly and honestly.

40. Xiè – Taking Apart

A time for action, but it's important not to act in haste. Solve the problem ahead of you, put it behind you and get on with things. Resist the temptation to dwell on the past.

41. Sǔn – Diminishing

Cut back on spending but share what you have with others, even if it means making sacrifices. If you do this readily and share your resources wisely, all will be well. Be patient.

42. Yì – Increase

Luck is on your side and you can make plans in confidence that they will be successful. You may make mistakes, but they will turn out to your advantage.

43. Quài – Breakthrough

Take precautions against possible losses and they will be kept to a minimum. Be firm without being pushy and try to cultivate friendships, for they will blossom.

44. Gòu – Meeting

Be resolute, stand your ground and don't give in whatever you do. Now is not the time to sign contracts or make agreements.

45. Cuì – Gathering Together

Sincerity and openness will help to make your relationship especially harmonious now. Keep a guard on your tongue. There may be a struggle ahead. If you feel that you are on your own with regard to a project, it is best to ask for help.

46. Shēng – Ascending

Although progress might be slow, at least you are going forwards. The help of a professional could be beneficial at the moment.

47. Kùn – Oppression

Things are difficult, but you need to stay calm and act correctly. You may have to dig deep into your reserves to overcome problems that arise.

48. Jĭng – The Well

Things are looking up, but nothing lasts forever! Insincerity on your part could have disastrous consequences. Excellent judgement regarding a situation or another person may be called for now. Stay on guard.

49. Gé – Revolution

Two forces are in conflict, each trying to destroy the other. There are opportunities for major changes ahead, but be alert and make sure the ground is well prepared. Proceed with care.

50. Dǐng – The Cauldron

Lots of little matters seem to be conspiring to get you down at the moment – equipment goes wrong, plans run late. Life soon picks up and things start to go well again. Don't forget to keep the material and spiritual aspects of your life in balance.

51. Zhèn – Thunder

The road ahead is rocky, but if you stay calm and proceed with care it will be smooth before too long. You may receive some bad news, but it might not have lasting significance.

52. Gèn – Mountain

If you maintain a low profile, problems that loom may well pass you by. Avoid taking risks. If you enjoy meditating, this is a good time for it; if you have never tried it, this is the best time to start.

53. Jiàn – Growth

Deal with things as they crop up and don't try to force the pace whatever you do.

54. Guī Mèi – Marrying Maiden

You may have been aiming too high – trim your sails and you won't regret it. Don't overdo things. Remember it's always darkest before the dawn.

55. Fēng – Abundance

Good fortune and luck shine upon you. Worries are a thing of the past for the moment.

56. Lǔ – Travelling

Movement and moving home are on the cards. With the changes this will bring, long-term commitments should be avoided. This is a time to make friends, but choose them wisely.

57. Xùn – Gentle

Be flexible. You may find that help comes from an unexpected source, so stick with any plans you have made.

58. Duì – The Joyous

Good news and good fortune come your way. You could be asked to enter into a partnership – work with the people who make the offer.

59. Huàn – Dispersal

A time for reason and taking the middle path. Friends from the past could resurface – if they do, strong bonds may be formed with them.

60. Jié – Limitation

You will probably be feeling shackled in some way, but if you remain calm you will soon be free and ready to take advantage of new opportunities that present themselves.

61. Zhōng Fú – Centre Returning

Favoured results should come from properly judged communications. Plans made now for the future will flourish.

62. Xiǎo Guò – Small Surpassing

Take care to ensure that you do not exceed your abilities or make promises and commitments you can't keep. Don't overspend at this time. It is best to stay realistic about what you can achieve. Tread carefully and attend to the smaller details of a project.

63. Jì Jì – After Completion

Celebrate your achievements but resist the temptation to sit back and rest just because you have been successful. This is a good time to reinforce the gains you have made. A new chapter awaits.

64. Wèi Jì – Before Completion

Don't make a move until you are certain the time is right and even then proceed with caution. Think long and hard before getting involved in something new, as you may come to regret it later.

NUMEROLOGY

THE MAGIC OF NUMBERS

PYTHAGORAS OF SAMOS asserted that numbers were the essence of all things. Each number, he taught his students at his school at Croton in Italy in the sixth century BCE, had its own quality and unique vibration. Pythagoras' combination of mathematics and mysticism inspired numerous schools and philosophies through the ages and combined with other systems, such as astrology and the kabbalah, to produce the numerology we practise today. As the meaning of numbers underpins all symbolic systems of divination, it is useful to understand the basic qualities of each one.

As with all symbolic systems, the meanings assigned to numbers can vary from one culture or school of thought to another, so it is worth exploring a range of systems to see how the different meanings compare.

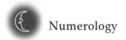
Numerology tends to be concerned with the numbers one to nine, from which all other numbers are formed. All numbers above 9 are separated into individual component numbers, which are then added up. Therefore 23 is broken down into 2 and 3; and 2 + 3 = 5.

Zero is not treated as a number in numerology terms. It can be understood as the great void out of which the number 1 emerges. Zero cannot be added to or subtracted from another number. Thus, the number ten exists as a composite of the number one (1 + 0 = 1).

We each have a variety of numbers that represent our personality, life purpose and various other elements. These numbers can be derived from our names, birth dates, addresses and other significant personal details. Sometimes we may not relate to the meaning of one or more of these numbers – this is perhaps because we are more conscious of another number which is more dominant in our personalities. It is helpful to calculate each one and see how it may be working in our lives and how we might better utilise its qualities.

THE BIRTH NUMBER

This number is derived from a person's date of birth and is thought to reveal his or her natural qualities, appearance and abilities. To calculate the birth number, write down your date of birth in numerical form and add up the digits until the sum is reduced to a single number. For example, a person born on 16 November 1981 has a birth number of 1, calculated as follows:

16/11/1981

$1 + 6 + 1 + 1 + 1 + 9 + 8 + 1 = 28$

As a composite number, 28 is broken down into $2 + 8 = 10$
And 10, as a composite number, is broken down into $1 + 0 = 1$

The destiny number

This number is derived from a person's full name and is used to indicate his or her life purpose.

The destiny number is calculated by assigning a number from 1–9 to each letter of the alphabet in consecutive order (see table below).

To calculate your destiny number, write down your full name, including any middle names. Then use the table to check the numerical quality of each letter and note it down. Add up these digits until a single number is reached. See the example below:

Michael Mitchell Johnstone

$4 + 9 + 3 + 8 + 1 + 5 + 3 + 4 + 9 + 2 + 3 + 8 + 5 + 3 + 3 + 1 + 6 + 8 + 5 + 1 + 2 + 6 + 5 + 5 = 109 = 1 + 0 + 9 = 10 = 1 + 0 = 1$

TABLE OF THE NUMERIC QUALITIES OF THE ENGLISH ALPHABET								
1	2	3	4	5	6	7	8	9
A	B	C	D	E	F	G	H	I
J	K	L	M	N	O	P	Q	R
S	T	U	V	W	X	Y	Z	

NUMBER MEANINGS

Number:

Planetary association: the Sun

Keywords: individuality, leadership, new beginnings, inexperience, energy

As the first number, arising out of the chaos of nothingness, 1 represents new beginnings, breaks with the past and stores of energy with which to start new projects. Associated with the Sun, a symbol of masculinity, the number 1 is linked with assertiveness, individuality and leadership.

People with this birth number are often striking in appearance, with a remarkable mane of hair, a lean, athletic body and glowing skin. They tend to be lively and have a healthy, active lifestyle.

As it is an early number, 1 may lack maturity and experience. However, the number's quality of enthusiasm, combined with an eagerness to learn and grow, more than compensates for this.

Number:

Planetary association: the Full Moon

Keywords: intuition, sensitivity, relationship, cooperation, balance

The number 2 represents relationships with others and the union of opposites. There is a desire to connect with people and to foster balanced and harmonious relationships. Linked with the Moon, a symbol of femininity, 2 brings strong intuition, the power of deep thought and sensitivity. People with this birth number can be easily affected and influenced by those around them. They are often pale skinned, have a sensitivity to bright sunshine and tend to feel liveliest at night. They often have a delicate physique and may be easily swayed. They may be so quietly spoken that people have to strain to hear what they are saying.

This number can also indicate a lack of self confidence and a tendency to place one's own needs aside in an effort to cooperate with others. In these situations, balance and moderation must be restored.

Number:

Planetary association: Mercury

Keywords: intelligence, curiosity, mental activity, creativity, self-development, sociability

A mystical number in many cultures, 3 is thought to have been created by the union of 1 (the Sun) and 2 (the Moon). People with the birth number 3 are usually highly intelligent, creative and good problem solvers. This makes them highly effective at school and in the workplace. Number 3 individuals enjoy learning and tend to be enrolled on one course of training after another.

People with this birth number tend to have a lean physique and lots of nervous energy to burn. They talk quickly and love to take part in debates with others.

The number 3 indicates a sociable, outgoing personality. However, 3s need to keep their minds active to avoid becoming bored and apathetic. They also require a great deal of freedom to be able to go wherever their curiosity takes them.

Number:

Planetary association: the Earth

Keywords: stability, contentment, practicality, habit, reliability, tenacity

The birth number 4 represents stability and contentment. People with this birth number are practical, have a strong respect for natural laws and know how to work within their limitations to succeed. They are industrious and enjoy hard work and the rewards it brings. They tend to have strong, stocky physiques and derive a great deal of satisfaction from physical activity.

They often have strong opinions and can be highly critical of others as well as themselves, which sometimes affects their confidence. But they are trustworthy and make reliable friends.

Number:

Planetary association: Mars

Keywords: action, will, power, courage, desire, restlessness, risk-taking

The birth number 5 represents the human will. People born with this number are mentally and physically active and always on the move. They have lots of energy and drive and follow their heart's desires with courage and persistence until they have achieved whatever it is that they set out to do.

They often have a muscular physique and because of their constant hurrying and scurrying, they tend not to put on weight. They enjoy physical activity and are often sexually irresistible! People with this birth number are usually cheerful and fun to be around, but they may lack patience and sensitivity and should take care not to over-extend themselves and take unnecessary risks.

Number:

Planetary association: Venus

Keywords: harmony, love, beauty, balance, attraction, charm, friendship

The number 6 represents love, attraction, beauty and creativity. Those with this birth number tend to enjoy loving and fruitful relationships. They have pleasing manners and are charming, outgoing and friendly. They have excellent taste and seem instinctively to know what looks good. For this reason they make excellent artists and designers.

Blessed with attractive, bright eyes and beautiful features, their love of the good things in life might lead to a tendency to put on weight.

Although they are charming company, people born under this number can sometimes be introverted and may prefer to stay at home in the company of close friends and family rather than stray too far outside their comfort zone.

Number:

Planetary association: Jupiter

Keywords: faith, hope, optimism, meaning, exploration, adventure

There are 7 days in the week, 7 colours in the rainbow, 7 pillars of wisdom, 7 deadly sins – the number 7 has many magical associations and is often linked with fortune and luck. People born with this number are often friendly, optimistic and fun to be around. They are seekers after truth and adventure and like to explore new territory and expand their perspective.

While they tend to have attractive, jovial features, number 7s are sometimes so preoccupied with ideas and questions of meaning that they take little care of their physical appearance.

Those born under this number require a great deal of freedom to explore. They may avoid emotional commitment to others if this threatens to get in the way of their personal quest for meaning.

Number:

Planetary association: Saturn

Keywords: patience, maturity, discipline, responsibility, practicality, judgement

Associated with the planet Saturn, 8 is the number of wisdom and patience. People born with this number tend to be sensible, mature individuals with a realistic approach to life. They are highly disciplined and work hard to fulfil their responsibilities and achieve their ambitions. They can make excellent businesspersons and managers.

People born with the number 8 are often tall and lean and sometimes appear more mature than their years. They often have excellent judgement, but need to take care not to become too world-weary and should remember to keep an open mind.

Number:

Planetary association: the New Moon

Keywords: endings, completion, wisdom, understanding, compassion, community, connectedness

The number 9 signifies wisdom and understanding. It is the end of the cycle and, like all endings, represents wholeness and completion. Selfless, compassionate and sensitive to the needs of others, people born with this number are often found working in the caring professions, charities or in their local communities.

Those born under the number 9 pay little attention to appearances. They tend to dress simply to avoid drawing too much attention to themselves.

Number 9 individuals should remember to treat themselves with the same compassion that they extend to others and should try to avoid over-stretching themselves.

PALMISTRY

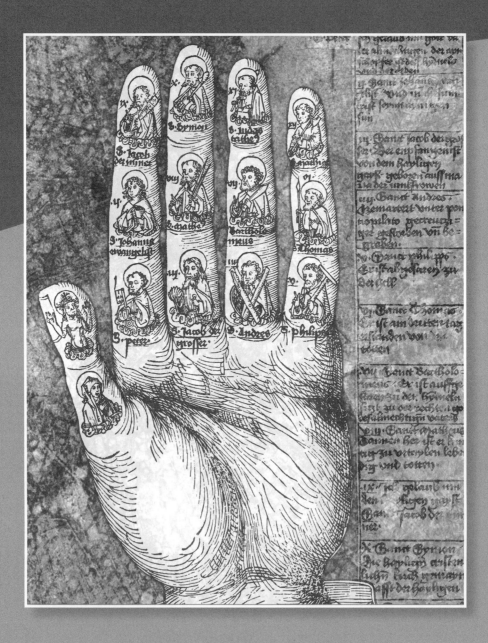

P ALMISTRY – ALSO KNOWN as palm-reading, chirology or cheiromancy – is the practice of reading the shapes, lines and other features of a person's hands to gain insight into their character, current experiences and what the future may hold for them.

While our basic hand shape remains with us through our lifetime, many features, including the lines, markings and spacing of the fingers, can change over time. A palm reading therefore tends to apply to the current moment and as we make choices to develop in new directions, so our hands start to adapt to reflect the changes in our lives.

ORIGINS

Like other forms of divination, palmistry is believed to have its origins in prehistory. The ancient Semitic texts contain references, as do the Indian Vedas and early Chinese manuscripts. We know that palmistry was popular in ancient Egypt, Persia and Greece. Homer is reputed to have written a 'Treatise on Palmistry', although the text has not survived.

The practice of hand reading is thought to have reached Europe around the twelfth century. It was possibly brought by Arab traders or by Europeans who had travelled to the East during the Crusades. While popular across Europe in medieval times, palmistry was one of a range of divinatory practices to be suppressed by papal decree and it was banned as sorcery during the reign of Henry VIII (r. 1509–47). Today, however, palmistry is one of the world's most popular forms of divination.

WHICH HAND?

As with all divinatory practices, there are many different schools of interpretation in palmistry today and numerous debates about which hand the palmist should consult in a reading. Often the left hand is taken to represent the past, the potential we are born with and the qualities we have inherited. The right hand represents the future, what we have made of our potential and the fate we are carving out for ourselves. Confusingly, however, these meanings sometimes apply only to men and may be reversed for women's hands! Often the dominant hand (the one you use to write with) is taken to represent a person's character and direction in life, while the other hand, known as the minor hand, indicates the person's background and inner potential.

Above: Homer was one of a number of ancient philosophers to practise palmistry.

PERFORMING A READING

Before carrying out a reading, the palmist will want to get to know the querent a little. An introductory chat can be very revealing. From this the palmist will be able to tell which of the querent's hands is dominant and whether the querent gesticulates while talking. The palmist will also look to see whether the hands are open and relaxed or clenched into a fist.

If the reading is given in person, the palmist will begin by taking the querent's hands and looking at their shape, texture and colour. The palmist will study the condition of the hands and fingernails, note any features or blemishes and look to see if the querent is wearing rings.

The palmist may do the reading by examining the hands physically or by taking photocopies or palm prints.

MAKING A PALM PRINT

To make a palm print (one for each hand), you will need:

- water-soluble ink for block printing (available from specialist art and craft shops)
- a smooth, hard surface on which to roll out the ink, such as a ceramic tile or linoleum block
- a hard rubber roller (available from specialist art and craft shops)
- a few sheets of paper
- a towel or similar

Squeeze some ink onto the tile (or other smooth surface) and move the roller back and forth over the ink until it is evenly coated. Now move the roller over the palm to be printed, ensuring the hand is evenly coated in a thin layer of ink from the tips of the fingers down to the wrist. Place a piece of paper on a soft but level surface (such as a towel on a table top), splay the fingers and thumb and carefully press the hand onto the paper. Roll it slightly so that all parts of the palm and the insides of the fingers and thumb have made contact with the paper. It may be worth trying this a few times on different sheets of paper to get the best possible print.

As there are bumps and depressions on every hand, it is normal for some areas not to make an impression on the paper. However, in some instances it may indicate parts of a person's character that are not being used to their maximum effect. Once you have made a satisfactory palm print, wash the ink off your hands and tools using hot water and soap (the ink may leave a faint stain, but will come off after a few washes).

TYPES OF HANDS

Just as no two people, not even identical twins, have identical fingerprints, so no two people have exactly the same hands. However, all hands have certain basic characteristics, which fall into general categories.

One of the first things a palmist may observe when studying a person's hands is their shape. The basic hand shapes are categorized into four elemental types, plus a fifth 'mixed' hand shape which may represent a person's temperament and can reveal a great deal about the subject of the reading.

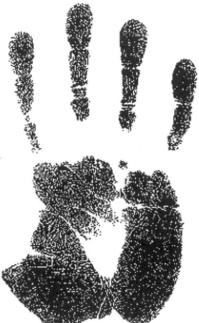

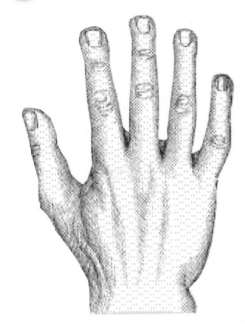

The Fire Hand

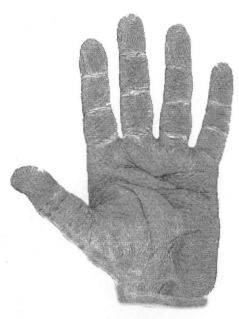

The Earth Hand

1. The Fire Hand

Fire hands tend to have a rectangular palm and fingers that are shorter than the length of the palm. The lines on the palm are often strong and numerous and have a busy look to them.

The fire hand indicates an energetic, restless temperament, a person who is full of excitement and enthusiasm and always looking for fresh challenges and opportunities to show his or her mettle. Fire hand individuals are often inventive, with a keen sense of curiosity that enables them to make discoveries and tread new ground. Full of courage and eager to impress and win the approval of others, they can be fearless risk-takers, but they may tend to bend the rules more than it is wise to do. They are fun and lively company, often the life and soul of the party, but may neglect their long-term needs in favour of short-term thrills.

2. The Earth Hand

Earth hands have a solid appearance, with broad, square palms and fingers that are about the same length as the palm. The nails and tips of the fingers are square-shaped and the skin is often thick and hardwearing.

People with earth hands tend to be practical, down-to-earth, hardy individuals with tremendous strength and stamina. They are known for their common sense and industriousness; they know how to get things done and are very handy around the home and garden! Often creatures of habit, they enjoy the comforts of home and make loyal, dependable companions. They are also usually very helpful individuals who can be relied upon in times of crisis. They can be dogged and persistent to the point of stubbornness and they are often cautious, preferring to stick with the familiar rather than experiment with something new.

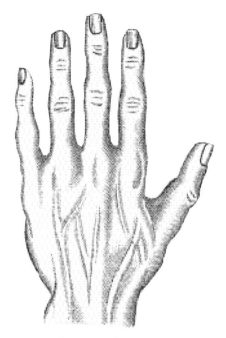

The Air Hand

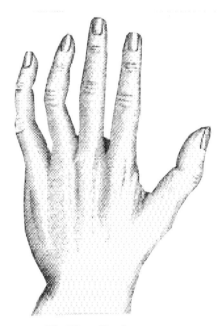

The Water Hand

3. The Air Hand

Air hands have square palms with long, boney fingers, sometimes with pronounced knuckles and joints. The fingers tend to have rounded or spatulate tips and the skin may have a tendency to dryness.

These hands are linked with rational thinking and the intellectual realm and often belong to teachers, philosophers and scientists. People with air hands tend to have an objective outlook on life and try to see the wider picture in every situation so that they can make a fair assessment of things. They are often clear communicators with lots of ideas and opinions they enjoy to share with others. Air hand types are quick learners and often good at solving problems and working out complex matters that require concentration. They can be very independent and tend to be made uncomfortable by excessive displays of public emotion. They need a lot of freedom to meet new people and explore their many interests.

4. The Water Hand

Water hands are graceful in shape with pointed, tapering fingers and a long, rectangular or oval palm. The lines on the hand tend to be fine and faint.

The water hand, also known as the psychic hand, indicates an person who follows his or her instincts and has an intuitive understanding of things that cannot be recognized by the rational mind alone. Usually linked with a high level of sensitivity and imagination, the water hand is prevalent among artists, musicians and those in the caring professions. People with water hands are often quite emotional and governed by their moods. They are daydreamers who wish and hope that their wildest fantasies will come true so that one day their every need will be fulfilled. They can be very trusting of others and hope for the best outcomes in life; they tend to take a passive approach to getting what they want, waiting for opportunities to come to them instead of actively pursuing them.

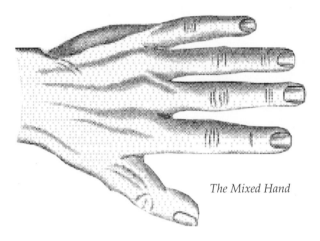

The Mixed Hand

5. The Mixed Hand

Often a hand shape does not fit any one of the main categories, but is a combination of two or more hand shapes. In this case, the meanings of the various shapes are synthesised.

THE DIGITS

In palmistry, our fingers and thumbs represent the way we express ourselves in the world.

LENGTH AND SHAPE

The palmist considers the length and shape of the querent's fingers, along with other characteristics, in order to refine their meaning further. A digit that is different from the others tends to describe dominant qualities in a person's personality.

Straight fingers indicate that the person expresses him or herself directly, with strength and ease, while crooked or twisted fingers suggest the opposite – that a person may struggle with direct expression and encounter obstacles or restrictions.

Long fingers generally indicate that the person is something of a perfectionist, while extra-long fingers show that he or she is prone to exaggeration. Short fingers suggest an impatient nature.

Flexible fingers and thumbs may indicate an easy-going, adaptable nature. Stiff fingers and thumbs, however, suggest stubbornness and an insistence on having everything one's own way.

Fingertips

Square fingertips indicate a practical, capable, down-to-earth nature – these individuals are hardworking and good with their hands. Rounded fingertips represent an easy-going and adaptable approach to life. Pointed fingertips indicate a sensitive nature – these individuals have a strong imagination and make excellent artists or writers.

Spatulate fingertips (where the tip of the finger is wider than the base) may suggest physically and mentally active individuals, whose dynamism means they tend to jump into things without careful planning.

THE PHALANGES

The phalanges are the sections between finger joints and represent different levels of consciousness. They are read from the tip down. The tip or first (1) phalange is concerned with the religious quest and personal philosophy; the middle or second (2) phalange corresponds to business and material concerns; and the bottom or third (3) phalange represents a person's basic needs and desires.

THE THUMB

The thumb is the most important digit in palmistry. Ruled by the planet Mars, it represents willpower, personal effectiveness and decision-making abilities. When the thumb is strong and substantial in size, it suggests that the person needs to assert his or her power and authority and exercise the will to achieve what he or she desires. If the thumb is small, curled or kept tucked into the palm it can denote a sense of subordination to the will of others and a deep frustration at not being able to assert one's own desires.

The size and condition of the thumb

A strong, thick thumb suggests a person has the capacity to deal with whatever life throws in his or her direction and is not afraid to battle with or confront others when required. People with longer thumbs (which reach at least halfway up the bottom phalange of the index finger) may find themselves frequently competing with others, whether in business,

sport or in love, as they enjoy the thrill of the chase! They need to feel that they have achieved something important through their talents and efforts. They can make excellent leaders, but may need to keep their tendency to control and dominate others in check!

People with short thumbs tend to be subordinate to stronger characters, lacking the will to resist them. This can lead to frustration and pent-up aggression. It is important for these people to find ways of releasing stress and channelling their desires in a constructive way to achieve their goals.

The thumb's phalanges

More information can be gleaned from the thumb's phalanges (see the diagram below) – the sections between the joints that are read from the tip down. The tip (1) phalange represents will; the lower phalange (2) represents logic. If the phalanges are about the same length it indicates a balance between rational, clear thinking and a developed sense of ambition, self-motivation and leadership. If the lower phalange is longer than the tip phalange, then its owner will probably think and reason a lot before taking a measured course of action, but may lack the willpower to put ideas into practice. If the upper phalange is longer, the person will actively pursue his or her desires, but may rush headlong into things without planning ahead and will frequently run into trouble as a result.

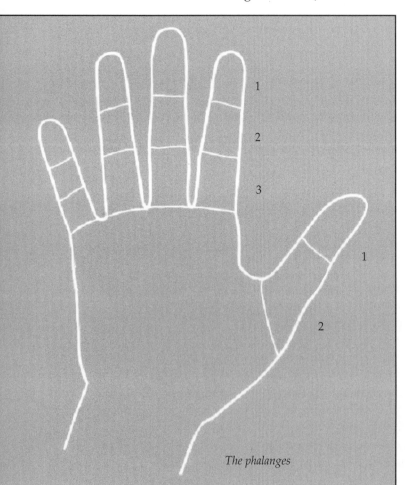

The phalanges

The angle of the thumb

When the hand is held naturally, the angle of the thumb to the index finger also yields significant information. If it is less than 45°, the individual has a tendency to be controlling. An angle of approximately 90° suggests that the person is a charming extrovert, outgoing and good company.

Thumb (Mars)

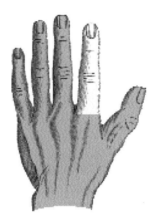

Index finger (Jupiter)

Middle finger (Saturn)

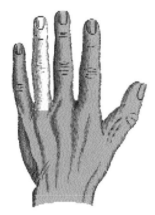

Ring finger (Sun or Venus)

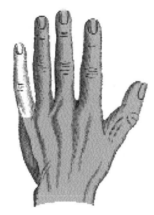

Little finger (Mercury)

THE INDEX FINGER

The index finger, also referred to as the forefinger or pointing finger, is ruled by Jupiter and indicates ambition and expansion.

A long index finger (longer than the ring finger) suggests self-confidence, a positive attitude and a highly developed sense of adventure. It may also indicate a strong ego. Its owner is ambitious and more than capable of achieving whatever he or she desires in the world. People with a long index finger may make fine leaders and intrepid adventurers. They have a tendency to exaggeration and going to extremes and don't always know when to stop.

A medium-length index finger shows that its owner is confident when required, but also capable of modesty and moderation.

A shorter index finger (in relation to the ring finger) indicates that the person may be shy, insecure, full of self-doubt and afraid of failure. Sometimes this can be masked by an overly confident exterior and desire to look important. However, such a mask is difficult to maintain and cracks will start to show if the individual is not honest with himself or herself. Genuine achievements through hard work and fulfilling one's responsibilities bring the greatest reward.

THE MIDDLE FINGER

The middle finger, ruled by Saturn, represents our duties and responsibilities in life.

A long, straight middle finger suggests strong ambition. These individuals work hard to get ahead, are reliable both at work and at home, fulfil their responsibilities to others and make exemplary citizens. They are excellent judges of situations, but may be overly judgemental of themselves and others and this can hold them back.

A medium-length middle finger indicates that the owner has the maturity to know when it is time to work and when it is time to play and uses moderation in everything.

A short middle finger (around the same length as the index and ring fingers) suggests a person who hates self-discipline and who refuses to follow routines or rules. Such people may lack ambition and direction in life and be unable to stick to any one course. They prefer to try out different things and avoid pressurising themselves.

THE RING FINGER

The ring finger is ruled by the Sun and Venus, and represents self-expression through our creative abilities.

A long ring finger (longer than the index finger) points to a charming and artistic nature. Sometimes it indicates a developed sense of fashion and style. These individuals are playful, with a strong sense of fun and desire for adventure. People with long ring fingers like to take risks (it can indicate a gambling streak). They like to be the centre of attention and enjoy receiving public recognition for their achievements. They may strive for the limelight of fame and celebrity.

A medium-length ring finger indicates a quietly confident personality with a more balanced and modest approach to self-promotion and a tendency to avoid taking unnecessary risks.

A short ring finger indicates that creativity and the imagination are not prominent qualities in a person's character (although other indications must be present in the hands to confirm whether this is indeed the case). Often these individuals will be shy and afraid of presenting themselves in public, preferring to remain in the background. They may lack confidence and be afraid to try things that involve risk.

THE LITTLE FINGER

The little finger, ruled by Mercury, is connected to mental abilities and powers of relating.

A long little finger (which reaches halfway up the top phalange of the ring finger) indicates intelligence and excellent communication skills. This belongs to a charismatic person with a quick wit and shrewd business abilities. It can also suggest a stronger than average sex drive and success in romantic pursuits.

A little finger that is medium in length shows moderate communication abilities and a person who is sufficiently confident that he or she can hold their own in social situations.

A short little finger (one which does not reach the top of the middle phalange of the ring finger) may indicate immaturity and a tendency towards gullibility and naivety. The individual may be shy and lack the ability to communicate effectively. People with short little fingers often feel misunderstood and may prefer their own company, but their self-induced isolation can lead to loneliness.

A little finger that naturally stands separate from the other fingers indicates an independent thinker who needs lots of space and likes to do things in his or her own way.

WEARING RINGS

Wearing rings on certain fingers can highlight the qualities of those fingers for us and may suggest that we are seeking to strengthen and protect those qualities, whether consciously or not. If we wear many rings it may suggest that we are feeling insecure and need to protect ourselves with emotional armour.

Rings on fingers have the following associations (remember that their meanings are particular to each hand – the left hand tends to represent our inherent qualities and the right hand represents the outer expression of these qualities):

Thumb – shows a desire to control other people and situations.

Index finger – indicates a strong ego and desire to take charge. It may also mask a sense of inferiority and self-doubt.

Middle finger – suggests ambition and a desire for material gain. May also mask feelings of insecurity and instability.

Ring finger – the conventional finger for engagement and wedding rings, symbolising a creative and happy union. If a person is wearing other rings on this finger, it could indicate emotional or creative frustration.

Little finger – This can indicate difficulties in social or sexual expression.

FINGERNAILS

Fingernails can also be analysed in palmistry and for this reason it is helpful for the nails to be free from nail polish during the reading. Square nails can indicate an easy-going temperament, while broad nails suggest a strong character with an explosive temper. Fan-shaped fingernails are a sign of high levels of energy and stress. A gentle, kind nature is indicated by almond-shaped fingernails. Narrow nails may suggest an ungenerous, self-centred personality.

The nails may also indicate health problems. Dietary deficiencies may result in horizontal or vertical ridges forming in the nails. White spots appearing on the nails may be related to a zinc deficiency, but are more likely to be the result of an injury to the nail bed when the nail was forming.

THE MAJOR LINES OF THE PALM

The major lines on the palms of our hands represent our basic energies and drives. The three main lines found on almost every human palm are the head line, the heart line and the life line. The fourth most commonly found line is the fate line, although this is far less frequently found than the other three lines.

The major lines are fully formed by the time we are teenagers, although islands, forks and other features connected to them tend to alter over time.

The strength and depth of the lines indicates the levels of energy inherent in those areas of our lives. Weak lines signify low energy and high sensitivity, whereas deep, strong lines indicate a powerful life force directed in those areas.

If a particular line stands out as the strongest and deepest of all, this indicates that our energies are mainly channelled toward that particular area. The faintest lines represent areas where we find expression difficult; we may need to make extra effort in this regard. When the lines are all equal in strength, it suggests that our energies are distributed evenly and are well-balanced.

A missing line can indicate drives that a person finds difficult to access. He or she may compensate for this by developing certain qualities more strongly. For example, someone with a missing head line may have difficulty studying some subjects, but may be naturally brilliant at others. Alternatively, such people may study hard to stretch their minds in a certain way and end up excelling in a subject. We also sometimes develop relationships with people who are strong in the qualities we lack and who are able to express them more naturally.

Fragmented lines signify a break in the flow of energy represented by the line in question. In the heart line this may represent a relationship break-up; in the life line it can suggest a temporary health problem or a new lease of life or transformation of some kind.

Forks and branches represent possible changes in direction and may indicate choices that need to be made about which path to take.

The characteristics of the major lines on an individual's palm should be considered alongside the other features of the hands to get a more complete picture of how these drives find expression in our lives.

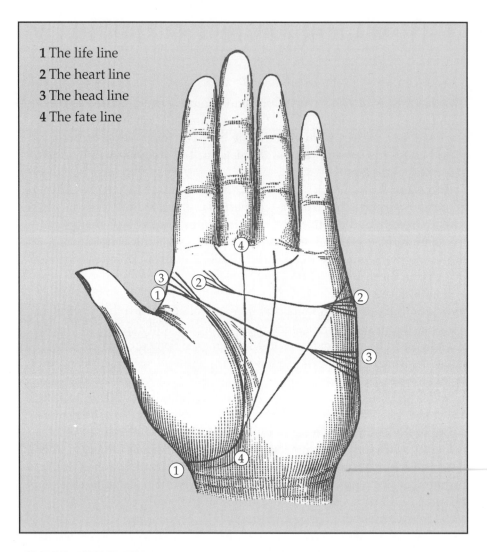

1 The life line
2 The heart line
3 The head line
4 The fate line

THE LIFE LINE

The life line represents our physical constitution, health, vitality and zest for life.

The life line begins on the thumb side of the palm (under the Mount of Jupiter) and curves downward towards the wrist, girdling the Mount of Venus (the fleshy area on the palm at the base of the thumb). The stronger the line and more pronounced the curve, the greater the energy in the life line.

A faint life line can be an indication of low vitality, depending on other indications in the hand. Lines that swing out from the main life line often describe a desire to travel and suggest life-changing experiences. Upward branches along the line represent achievements and may indicate that the individual has made a tremendous effort to get back on his or her feet after some sort of setback.

Splits along the line represent changes to our health and may indicate a new lease of life or new phase which the individual will embark on at a particular stage. The timing of this phase will depend on where the split appears in the line. The top of the line starts near the thumb and represents the time of our birth; the bottom of the line near the wrist indicates old age, the centre of the line middle age, and so on.

THE HEART LINE

The heart line represents our emotional energy and approach to love relationships. This line runs horizontally across the top of the palm, starting on the opposite side to the life line.

If the heart line is straight, the individual will be dispassionate and detatched from his or her emotions and may take time to form close relationships. A strongly curved heart line points to an individual who loves being in love and shows it, the sort person who takes the lead in any relationship.

A heart line that curves steeply toward the index and middle digits indicates strong sexual desires and passions. A heart line that ends under the middle finger denotes practicality in matters of the heart, but also may indicate that the individual is insecure and in need of constant reassurance from his or her partner.

Love affairs can be indicated by forks or branches emanating from the heart line. Branches ascending from the heart line will tend to be positive experiences and those descending tend to represent more challenging relationship encounters.

If there are lots of small lines branching from the heart line, the person will be friendly and gregarious and will have an active social life.

THE HEAD LINE

The head line represents our mental energy and powers of reasoning and concentration.

The head line runs horizontally between the life and heart lines and usually starts on or near the beginning of the life line. If the two lines have distinct starting points (which is usual) a well-balanced, independent nature is indicated. If their starting points overlap, dependence on others is indicated.

A long head line points to a person who thinks before acting; a short one to someone who is quick-thinking and decisive. A straight head line represents a person who may be highly rational but lacking in imagination. A slanting line indicates an imaginative and intuitive character. A line that curves steeply rather than slants downwards indicates lateral thinking.

Receptivity to new ideas is signified by the presence of lots of outward branches from the head line. If they point toward the Mount of Jupiter (see diagram on page 149), leadership qualities are indicated. If they point to the Mount of Saturn, a hardworking nature is suggested and the person concerned may be a talented researcher, accountant or banker.

Artistic achievement is indicated by branches that point towards the Mount of Apollo. Branches pointing towards the Mount of Mercury can indicate a career in business or communications. Any lines that branch downwards may suggest periods of depression, but branches that run to the Mount of the Moon can represent success in the arts or other creative pursuits.

The area between the heart and head lines is known as the quadrant. A particularly wide space or quadrant between these lines is suggests a confident and impulsive nature. A small quadrant represents lack of confidence in one's own opinions and decision-making ability and an individual who is inclined to be concerned about what others think.

THE FATE LINE

The fate line represents our drive and desire to achieve. It marks the direction in which we are heading.

The fate line runs from the bottom area of the palm upwards, usually towards the Mount of Saturn, and represents career, marriage and the family unit. A long, straight fate line suggests a person has a strong sense of direction in life and implies that the path to attaining their goals will be smooth and steady.

People with missing, weak or fragmented fate lines may have an unsettled path through life and might have to change jobs several times before they work out what they want to do and find their niche.

A fate line beginning at the Mount of Venus (see diagram on page 149) suggests that romantic matters will be bound up with the person's ambitions and career choices. A fate line that reaches the middle finger suggests that the subject will remain active until old age. A fate line that begins at the head line suggests that academic effort has played an important part in the person achieving success in life. A line that stops at the heart line may be an indication of a sexual indiscretion that will affect a person's career.

THE MINOR LINES

While most of us will have the major palm lines engraved on our hands, many of us will not have all the minor lines.

In general, if there are few lines in the palm of the hand this indicates an easy-going character who likes a simple, uncomplicated life and approaches one thing at a time to avoid undue stress or confusion. These individuals prefer to stay calm and avoid confrontation as much as possible.

A busy hand with many lines belongs to a person who has a range of activities on the go at once and who enjoys keeping active. These people sometimes thrive on stress and drama.

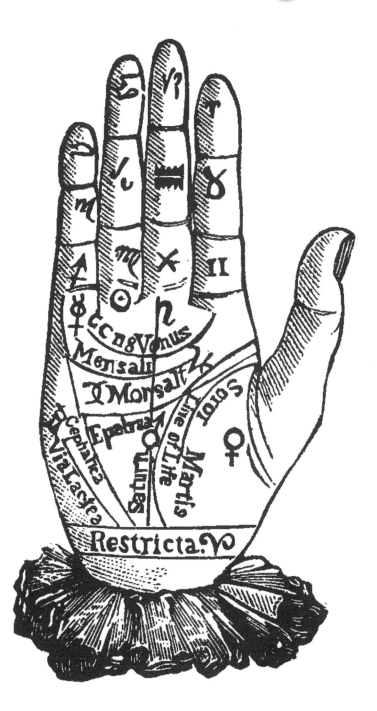

Planetary and zodiacal diagram of the right hand, from Wehman's *Witches' Dream Book*, New York, 1885.

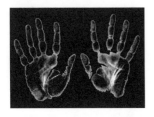

THE SUCCESS LINE

Often called the Line of Apollo, the success line runs vertically from the palm towards the middle finger. It represents the importance of fame, fortune and success to the individual. If there is a break in the line, this indicates a period of struggle in achieving one's dreams.

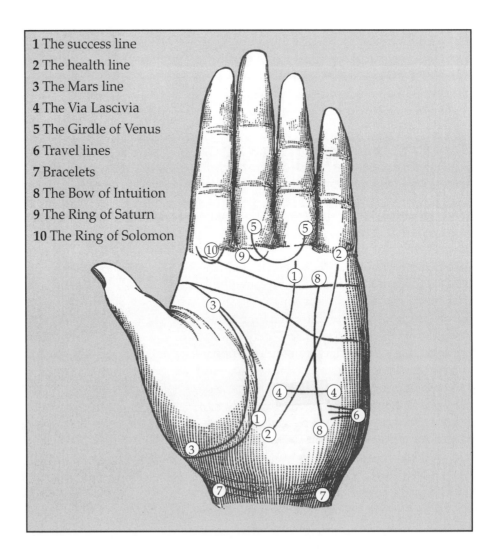

1 The success line
2 The health line
3 The Mars line
4 The Via Lascivia
5 The Girdle of Venus
6 Travel lines
7 Bracelets
8 The Bow of Intuition
9 The Ring of Saturn
10 The Ring of Solomon

THE HEALTH LINE

The health line, sometimes called the Line of Mercury, represents an overdeveloped concern for health and, possibly, hypochondria. A health line that starts close to the Mount of Venus (see diagram on page 149) suggests a tendency towards digestive problems; a long health line implies that worries may aggravate stress-related illnesses such as ulcers.

THE MARS LINE

Sometimes a second line runs parallel to the inside of the life line (nearer the thumb) – this is known as the Mars line. It suggests that our health and wellbeing have an extra layer of protection, which can be helpful in times of low vitality or ill health. The Mars line may also represent a close family member or friend who looks after our wellbeing.

THE VIA LASCIVIA

A horizontal line running across the Mount of the Moon (see diagram on page 149) represents a robust constitution and good health for those who have it. It may also suggest that the individual suffers from allergies to certain foods or substances.

THE GIRDLE OF VENUS

The Girdle of Venus is a semi-circular line above the heart line which stretches across the mounts of Saturn and Apollo (see diagram on page 149). It may suggest increased sensitivity and deep feelings and emotions.

TRAVEL LINES

Running horizontally from the outer edge of the hand and across the Mount of the Moon (see diagram opposite), these short lines indicate important journeys in a person's lifetime or may indicate an interest in expanding one's horizons and learning about distant regions and cultures.

BRACELETS

These are the horizontal lines extending across the base of the palm around the wrist. A number of parallel bracelets brings the blessing of a long and happy life.

THE BOW OF INTUITION

This is a very unusual line found opposite the thumb, starting at the Mount of the Moon and curving up towards the Mount of Mercury (see diagram on page 146). It indicates intuition and a prophetic ability.

THE RING OF SATURN

Another rare line, seen as a small arc below the middle finger, the Ring of Saturn indicates a reclusive nature and tendency towards miserliness.

THE RING OF SOLOMON

People who are well respected for their common sense often have this line, which runs around the base of the index finger.

THE MOUNTS

The raised pads on the hands are called 'mounts' or 'mounds'. The most significant mounts are those of the Moon, Mars Lower and Venus.

THE MOUNT OF THE MOON

Located at the outside edge of the lower section of the palm, the Mount of the Moon is concerned with the unconscious realm, memories and the ebb and flow of emotions. If it is fleshy and pronounced, it indicates strong emotions and a vivid imagination, with a tendency towards introspection. Sensitivity and a perceptive nature are indicated by a normal-sized Mount of the Moon, while people with a flat mount tend to be unimaginative and insensitive to their own needs as well as to those of others.

THE MOUNTS OF MARS

Found on the outside edge of the hand, above the Mount of the Moon, the Lower Mount of Mars represents motivation. If it is large, there is a tendency towards aggression and discord, while a depressed Mount of Mars may represent cowardice. A normal Mars Lower suggests courage,

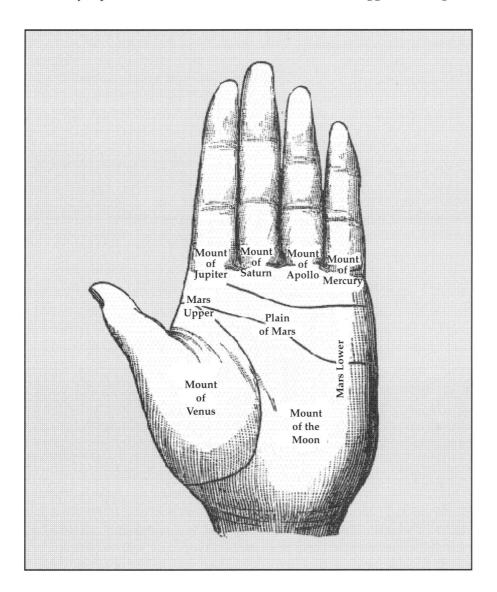

a person who will pick up the gauntlet and fight for a cause he or she believes in.

The Upper Mount of Mars is on the opposite side of the palm, sandwiched between the mounts of Venus and Jupiter. A large Upper Mount of Mars is a sign of tremendous energy and enthusiasm. Moral courage can be indicated by a normal Upper Mount of Mars and cowardice by a flat or depressed mount.

THE PLAIN OF MARS

The Plain of Mars is in the hollow of the centre of the palm. If the lines around it are distinct and unbroken, the subject probably enjoys good health and prosperity and can look forward to a long life. Optimism is indicated by a flat plain, but if it is hollow, then individual may lack drive and ambition.

THE MOUNT OF VENUS

Located at the base of the thumb, this mount is connected with love and harmony in relationships. Fleshy and well-developed, it suggests a strong sex drive and sensuality and a desire for a family. Sitting high and soft to the touch, it indicates excitability and fickleness. If it is depressed or flat, then the individual may have a low sex drive (depending on other features, such as the condition of the heart line).

THE MOUNT OF MERCURY

This is the mount of self-expression, of travel and of business interests. A large Mount of Mercury suggests a good sense of humour and a warm, receptive nature. Powers of persuasion, subtlety and quick-thinking are indicated by a normal-sized mount. But if it is flat, then the subject could be shy and a bit of a loner.

THE MOUNT OF APOLLO

Situated at the base of the ring finger, this mount is related to personal success, charm and creativity. High-achievers and people in the limelight often have a pronounced Mount of Apollo, although they can be prone to extravagance and egotism. An underdeveloped Mount of Apollo can indicate an underachiever (but this also depends on other features in the hands).

THE MOUNT OF SATURN

Located at the base of the middle finger, an over-prominent Mount of Saturn suggests a person who is serious and judgemental of himself or herself and others. If the mount is flat or undeveloped, the individual may lack goals and ambition (depending on other signifiers in the hands).

THE MOUNT OF JUPITER

This mount, if well-pronounced, suggests that its owner is confident of success. If the mount is especially high, then arrogance is indicated. A flat, undeveloped Mount of Jupiter indicates laziness and a dislike of authority.

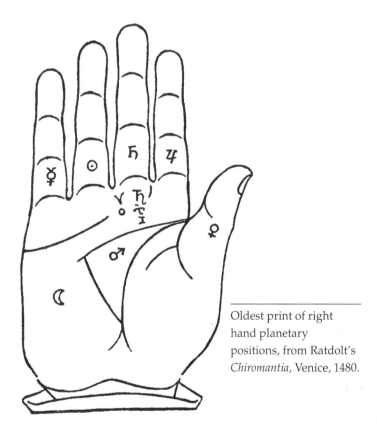

Oldest print of right hand planetary positions, from Ratdolt's *Chiromantia*, Venice, 1480.

CASTING THE RUNES

RUNES ARE STONE, wood or clay pieces on which mystical symbols have been engraved. The symbols derive from ancient Germanic alphabets. Runes have been used for divination purposes for thousands of years. Their popularity has seen a revival in the last century and they continue to be used as talismans and for divination today.

ORIGIN OF THE RUNES

The word rune means 'secret' or 'whisper' in the languages from which it stems. Casting the runes dates back several thousand years to the ancient Germanic and Scandinavian regions of northern Europe. With their roots in Norse mythology, the runic symbols represent birds, animals and other images from the world of nature, although their original meanings are now lost to us.

Runes were dedicated to Odin, the supreme deity in the Norse pantheon, and are associated with travel, healing, communication and divination. According to myth, in his search for enlightenment, Odin hung himself upside down on Yggdrasil, the World Tree, and impaled himself on his own spear for nine days. As Odin stared at the ground below, the rune stones hidden in Yggdrasil's roots revealed themselves to him.

The legend probably derives from the mythology of the Volsungr, a tribe of priest-magicians and guardians of the ancient forests, who used an early form of runes (Ur Runes) to divine the future. At the end of the last Ice Age, the Volsungr ventured southwards, bringing their knowledge and runic symbols with them as they moved through Scandinavia and into central Europe.

By Roman times, the runes had evolved into the Elder and Younger Futhark, which were regional variations of the runic alphabet. The Roman historian Tacitus, writing in Germania in the first century CE, described a runic ceremony during which a branch was cut from a nut-bearing tree and cut into small pieces (rune slips) on which runic symbols were marked. These rune slips were cast onto a white cloth and interpreted by a priest. However, little evidence remains of how runes were used in this early period of history.

Whenever a journey had to be made, the runes were cast to establish the most propitious time to set out. Runes therefore followed the trade routes across Europe and into Iceland, Greenland, Russia, Turkey, Greece and North Africa. They may even have found their way to the Americas, as evidenced by the runic carvings found on monuments and other artefacts discovered in these regions.

By around the fifth century CE, the runes had gained in popularity in Anglo-Saxon England, where new symbols were introduced. However, the practice of rune-casting gradually died out, not just in Britain but in other parts of the world as the Christian religion took hold.

In the nineteenth and twentieth centuries, the rise of German nationalism and a revival of interest in Teutonic folklore led to the renewal of interest in the runes. However, during the 1930s and 1940s the German folklore revival came to be linked with Nazism and the runes once again fell into disfavour.

With the renaissance of neo-paganism and New Age practices in recent decades, runes have once again become popular, not only for divining the future and increasing wisdom and self-knowledge, but also as talismans.

THE RUNES IN CURRENT TIMES

The runes in popular use today are the Germanic Elder Futhark set, which consists of 24 characters divided into three sets, or aettirs. Each aettir is named after a Norse deity. The first set is dedicated to Freya, the goddess of love, lust, war and death. The second set is named for Hagal, the guardian of the remaining gods and goddesses in the Norse pantheon. Tiwaz, god of justice and law, war and the sky, rules the third aettir.

The runes are understood to have one meaning when upright and an opposite meaning when reversed (upside down) or *merkstave* (lying

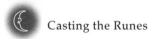

sideways or off centre). *Merkstave* means 'dark stick' and implies a negative impediment. Nine of the 24 runic characters appear the same whether upright or reversed and can only be read as upright or *merkstave*. The remaining 15 can be drawn upright, reversed or *merkstave*.

A reversed or *merkstave* rune is read in relation to its intrinsic meaning and its position in the spread. When a rune is upside down or *merkstave*, it represents an area that needs more attention and which can be used more positively by the querent.

Runes can help us look deeply into our inner selves, allowing us to pinpoint fears and desires and highlight the hidden factors that will shape the future. They describe positive and negative influences, indicate ways to maximise the former and minimise the latter and help us to make constructive choices for the future.

USING RUNES

Runes made of stone, wood, clay and other materials are available at specialist shops, but many people prefer to make their own rune slips and find that the simple, angular shapes of the symbols are relatively easy to carve. As with other tools used for divination purposes, runes should be kept in a special bag or pouch and stored in a safe place when not in use. They should be handled only by the diviner and the querent.

Contemporary rune sets often contain one blank rune. Although not all diviners use this rune, those who do refer to it as Wyrd and interpret it as a sign that all possibilities are open. The querent must work towards achieving the desired outcome, but outside influences are beyond his or her control and mean that the matter can go either way. Being blank, Wyrd cannot be reversed or *merkstave*.

Today, there is a range of names for each rune. On the following pages, the meanings and associations of the 24 runes are listed, together with the two most commonly used names for each one.

THE MEANING OF THE RUNES

FREYA'S AETTIR

Fehu / Feoh

Meaning: cattle
Keyword: prosperity

This rune represents prosperity and material gain, probably in the form of reward for past efforts. It signifies foresight and fertility and, as an energetic rune, speaks of new opportunities and social success.

Reversed or *merkstave* it signifies that achievements, such as status or self-esteem, may be lost. It also indicates failure, perhaps brought about by greed or bad judgement.

As a talisman, this rune is used to achieve a goal, gain promotion or bring luck to a new business venture.

Uruz / Ur

Meaning: bison
Keyword: strength

The right way up, this rune of strength, courage and overcoming obstacles suggests that what seemed to be a loss is in fact an opportunity in disguise. It speaks of action, good health and promises wisdom and the chance to gain deeper insight.

Reversed or *merkstave*, it suggests a character too easily led or influenced by others, a quality that can result in lost opportunity. Drawn reversed, it also threatens ill health, inconsistency, ignorance, callousness, brutality and violence.

As a talisman, this rune is used to strengthen the will and increase sexual potency.

Thurisaz / Thor

Meaning: thorn
Keyword: challenge

This rune represents change. It may signal the approach of a destructive force or conflict, which can be overcome if instincts are heeded.

Reversed or *merkstave*, Thurisaz warns of vulnerability, leading to some sort of danger. It indicates betrayal and possibly describes a person with malicious intent.

As a talisman, this rune encourages study, meditation and the resolution of an unpleasant situation.

Ansuz / Oss

Meaning: one of the gods
Keyword: communication

This is a rune of inspiration, aspiration and communication, particularly with the gods. It encourages clear vision and increased intuition about what the future holds. It can also represent good health.

Reversed or *merkstave*, Ansuz indicates misunderstandings and negative expectations about the future, which will lead to a feeling of disillusionment. It also warns against vanity, arrogance and pomposity.

As a talisman, this rune is helpful for divination and in making wise decisions. It is also useful in developing leadership qualities.

Rado / Rit

Meaning: riding
Keyword: journey

This rune represents travel, be it a physical journey in the form of a holiday or other change of location or a journey of the mind through study and further education. It may even indicate a journey of the soul. It brings with it the chance to put things in perspective.

Reversed or *merkstave*, Radō suggests that a crisis is brewing or that there will be some sort of disruption. It also suggests that the querent feels caged in by present circumstances.

As a talisman, this rune brings protection to travellers. It encourages change and helps to gain perspective on matters.

Kenaz / Kaon

Meaning: torch
Keyword: wisdom

This rune is associated with inner guidance and illumination. It promises that light will be shone into dark places, bringing new discoveries and realisations. These will lead to positive change and the development of inner strength.

Reversed or *merkstave*, it can represent weakness and negative influences – hopelessness, negativity and despair – that will cast a cloud over matters.

As a talisman, it can be used to strengthen inspiration and creativity and dispel anxiety and fear.

Gebo / Gifu

Meaning: gift
Keyword: generosity

Gebō represents exchanges, including contracts or exchanges of love, marriage and partnership. It suggests balance and equality.

While it cannot be reversed, when *merkstave* it warns of greed, imbalance of power, broken contracts, failed partnerships and loneliness.

As a talisman, Gebō is used to strengthen relationships, encourage fertility and bring good luck in all endeavours.

Wunjo / Wunna

Meaning: joy
Keyword: pleasure

Wunjō represents comfort, joy and pleasure, along with the promise of prosperity and harmony in relationships. Moderation and self-control will bring the greatest benefits.

Reversed or *merkstave*, this rune warns of sorrow, strife and a sense of alienation from others. It may represent delays, arguments and belligerent behaviour.

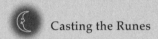
As a talisman, Wunjō inspires motivation and helps bring unfinished tasks to completion.

HAGAL'S AETTIR

Hagalaz / Hagal

Meaning: chaos
Keyword: change

Hagalaz, the Mother Rune, represents uncontrolled forces of nature which bring havoc and disruption. It indicates a time of trials and tests. Crises will lead to the long-awaited completion or closure of a matter.

While it cannot be reversed, when *merkstave* the rune can herald destruction as well as loss of power and a period of hardship, loss and stagnation.

As a talisman, Hagalaz removes unwanted influences and is used to break destructive cycles.

Naudhiz / Naut

Meaning: need
Keyword: constraint

This rune represents constraints, delays and obstacles that stand in our way. We are required to face our fears and accept the things we cannot change. We may be required to do without something we need for a period of time.

Reversed or *merkstave*, it suggests that freedom will be restricted and self-control is required in a matter.

As a talisman, this rune is used to bring fulfillment of our needs and encourages a positive outcome in a matter.

Isaz / Is

Meaning: ice
Keyword: stillness

This rune is known for reinforcing and underlining the message of those around it. It decribes challenges and blocks to creativity. Matters may be at a standstill for the moment; it is a time to look inwards until matters move on again.

While it cannot be reversed, when *merkstave* it represents treachery and deceit and warns the querent to beware of being trapped or ambushed by other people.

As a talisman, it can be used to suspend problems and difficulties and bring some welcome relief.

Jera / Yer

Meaning: year
Keyword: harvest

This is the rune of the harvest, when the results of previous efforts can be gathered in. It heralds a happy period of peace and prosperity and suggests a possible breakthrough in a matter that has been dormant for a while.

While it cannot be reversed, when *merkstave* it warns of an unexpected reversal of fortune which may result in major life changes. Conflict may be unavoidable in arriving at these changes.

As a talisman, this rune is used to encourage change and fertility.

Eiwaz / Yr

Meaning: yew
Keyword: endings

The yew tree represents the cycle of death and rebirth and Eiwaz indicates that matters will come to a natural ending, leading to new beginnings. It also represents changes and turning points.

While this rune cannot be reversed, when *merkstave* it warns of confusion and an inability to overcome obstacles.

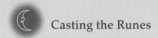

As a talisman, it can bring about huge changes or show the way to surmount difficulties.

Perthro / Peorth

Meaning: dice cup
Keyword: initiation

This rune suggests deep transformative powers are at work and have yet to be revealed. Mysteries, secrecy and psychic abilities are indicated. A chance may be taken in order to change direction.

While it cannot be reversed, when *merkstave* it warns of harmful addictions, a sense of disconnection from others and a loss of faith in the future.

As a talisman, it helps in the practice of divination because it enhances psychic ability. It is also used to ease pain in childbirth.

Algiz / Aquizi

Meaning: elk
Keyword: protection

This rune suggests that help will come from an unexpected source to ward off a threat of some kind. Algiz also encourages us to channel our energies for the benefit and protection of loved ones.

Reversed or *merkstave* it is a sign that hidden dangers lie ahead and ill health may be indicated. We are warned to consider advice received with care, as it may not be in our best interests.

As a talisman, Algiz is used for protection and to help build defences.

Sowilo / Sig

Meaning: sun
Keyword: wholeness

The rune of potential success, energy and expansion, Sōwilō promises that goals will be achieved and honours bestowed. Humility and restraint should be exercised.

While it cannot be reversed, when *merkstave* it indicates the receipt of bad advice leading to the failure to meet goals, resulting in despair and blame. It is important to accept responsibility for mistakes and move on.

As a talisman, this rune boosts energy levels and increases strength, positivity and enthusiasm.

TIWAZ'S AETTIR

Tiwaz / Tiu

Meaning: star
Keyword: justice

Honour, justice, victory and authority are indicated by this rune. It points to a willingness to make a sacrifice in order to achieve your goals. Victory and success are on the horizon, perhaps in a legal matter.

Reversed or *merkstave* it can indicate exhaustion and stagnation, bad judgement and a tendency to be overly critical in a matter. Strife and conflict can lead to difficulties in communication and a separation of some sort.

As a talisman, Tīwaz brings justice, protection and victory. It can strengthen the will and help wounds to heal.

Berkanen / Birca

Meaning: birch
Keyword: rebirth

Berkanen is the rune of birth, fertility, growth and regeneration. It represents the springtime, bringing the promise of growth and new beginnings. A fertile idea or match is indicated. The rune also suggest a new venture will be successful and bring prosperity.

Reversed or *merkstave*, this rune indicates domestic troubles and difficulties with loved ones. It warns against carelessness and loss of control.

As a talisman it can be used to aid fertility and regeneration, heal wounds, bring about a good harvest and make a fresh start.

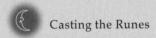

Ehwaz / Eh

Meaning: horse
Keyword: harmony

Harmonious relations, teamwork, trust and loyalty are represented by this rune. Ehwaz indicates travel and the use of transportation of some kind to achieve your goals. It heralds change for the better, brought about by steady progress. It suggests that a partnership or match in marriage will be an ideal one. It also confirms the meaning of the runes around it in a reading.

Reversed or *merkstave* it indicates a craving for change of some sort, a feeling of restlessness or of being confined in a situation not of your own making. It can also presage reckless haste, disharmony, mistrust and betrayal.

As a talisman, it is used to bring harmony in relationships and to improve communication and teamwork.

Mannaz / Man

Meaning: man
Keyword: humanity

Mannaz represents friends, enemies and social order. When this rune appears, some sort of aid or cooperation can be expected in a situation. Mannaz is concerned with human qualities of intelligence, forethought, culture and civilisation.

Reversed or *merkstave* the rune indicates the onset of depression, hopelessness and a lack of foresight. It warns of the danger of falling prey to cunning and manipulative behaviour. If you do, help cannot be found.

As a talisman, it is used to strengthen groups and support social endeavours and humanitarian causes.

Laguz / Lagu

Meaning: water
Keyword: life force

Laguz is a rune of the sea, of water's ebb and flow and the healing power of renewal. It emphasises imagination and psychic matters, dreams and fantasies, the mysteries of the unknown. It hints at the importance of what is hidden or belongs to the underworld. Reversed or *merkstave* Laguz indicates a period of confusion in the subject's life. It suggests that he or she may be making bad decisions through poor judgement and may be suffering from lack of creativity or concerned that he or she is in a rut. At its worst, reversed or *merkstave* this rune presages insanity and obsession – being cast into such deep despair that unspeakable thoughts come to mind. As a talisman, Laguz enhances psychic abilities and helps those who wear or carry it to face their fears. It stabilises emotional disorders and helps to uncover what is hidden.

Ingwaz / Ing

Meaning: earth god
Keyword: people

Ingwaz is concerned with male fertility, gestation and internal growth. It represents common sense and simple strengths, building a home and caring for the family. It presages a period of rest and relaxation, when anxieties disappear, ongoing matters are resolved and you are free to move in a new direction.

While it cannot be reversed, when *merkstave* it brings impotence, wasted effort and hard work with little reward.

As a talisman, Ingwaz is used to aid fertility and growth, encourage good health and restore balance.

Othala / Odal

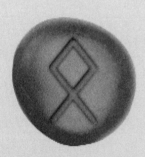

Meaning: homestead
Keyword: heritage

This rune represents ancestry, inheritance and possessions. It can describe the house and home and objects that hold sentimental value. It can also indicate prosperity for your family or socal group. It protects against difficulties on journeys.

Reversed or *merkstave* it warns of being controlled by an external force and inheriting a harmful legacy for which one is held responsible.

As a talisman, Othala helps with the acquisition of property, bringing a project to a successful conclusion and strengthening family ties.

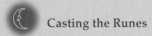

Dagaz / Dag

Meaning: day
Keyword: integration

Dagaz represent the dawn of new opportunities and breakthroughs, awareness and awakening. It promises that clarity will light up the subject's life and recommends that now is the time to embark on a new enterprise. Use your will to bring about desired change and your actions will lead to success, growth and release.

While it cannot be reversed, when *merkstave* it can presage completion and endings and may indicate that the subject is in danger of losing faith and hope in a matter.

As a talisman, it brings a renewed sense of hope, limitless possibilities, new ambitions and a positive outcome to any situation.

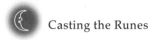

RUNIC SPREADS

The runes can be cast in several spreads, many of which are based on Tarot card spreads. In each case the querent must first focus on the question, whether it is regarding a specific matter – for example, should I marry X? – or a general situation – for example, what influences are strong in my life at the moment?

Perhaps the quickest and simplest of these is the one-rune spread. With this, the querent picks one rune at random from the bag or pouch in answer to a question.

The three-rune spread is also straightforward. With this, the querent focuses on the question to be answered and casts three runes. The first rune indicates the past, the second represents the present and the third reveals the future outcome of the matter.

The nine-rune method can help the querent gain a fuller impression of a matter and relies more strongly on intuition to interpret the spread. First the querent picks nine runes from the pouch at random. With the question in mind, he or she throws the runes onto a white cloth, large table top or other surface. The runes that fall face upwards can be read first; they describe the current situation. The runes lying in the centre of the spread describe that which is most relevant to the matter, and those scattered further from the centre represent more general influences.

The meanings of runes positioned next to one another are read together. If one rune is lying on top of another, it means that it is opposing or blocking the function of the rune beneath in some way. If a rune falls far from the rest or drops off the surface being used it may be ignored, but some diviners consider stray runes to have the greatest significance of all in a reading.

Ultimately, everything depends on the intuition of the diviner as to how the spread is read. The more experienced the diviner, the better able he or she will be to draw insight from the casting of the runes.

ASTROLOGY

Astrology is one of the most popular forms of fortune-telling today. It explores the symbolic correspondences between the position of planets, stars and other astronomical bodies and the events on Earth.

Like the other systems of divination explored in this book, astrology is used to develop wisdom and insight and to answer specific questions we may have about the future. It can be applied to the life of a person, a relationship, an animal, an object, event, new project or venture, a business, group, country, political event, idea, fashion or trend, the weather – in fact, anything under the sun!

A number of different astrological systems have developed in societies and cultures around the world. This section focuses on the astrology practised in the West today.

ORIGINS

Astrology as we know it today is the product of thousands of years of evolution. The roots of Western astrology can be traced back to early Mesopotamian culture, although its true beginnings are hard to ascertain. This is because, as with most forms of divination, they lie in prehistory.

The Sun, Moon, planets and stars are fundamental to our experience of living on Earth. It is thought that from the dawn of human consciousness humans have observed the movements of celestial bodies and assigned significance to them. As civilisations developed, astrology began to be used in relation to planting and agriculture, timing and calendars, rituals and religious traditions.

The earliest known astrological text was

written before 1600 BCE. *The Venus Tablet of Ammisaduqa*, part of a series of Babylonian tablets known as the *Enuma Anu Enlil*, recorded astrological omens and was used to predict the fate of whole nations. The ancient Greeks merged scientific observations, philosophies and mythologies with religious elements, which they brought to the Mesopotamian astrological system. One of astrology's most popular axioms, 'as above, so below', is based on the theory of *microcosm–macrocosm*, a principle central to many forms of divination. This philosophy states that the large scale (the cosmos) corresponds to the small scale (the individual human being); in this way, the events in the life of a person can be perceived in relation to the workings of the universe.

The Greek philosopher Empedocles (circa. 490-430 BCE) is credited with devising the theory of the four universal elements – earth, air, fire and water – which were later incorporated into the symbolic make-up of the zodiac and other mantic systems. Hippocrates (circa. 460-370 BCE) then related these four elements to the four humours of the human body and used this theory to develop a holistic method of healing. This method was later used in medical astrology and other forms of medical treatment that continued into the Middle Ages.

Both astrology and astronomy apparently reached their peak during Ptolemy's era (first century CE), flourishing in Rome until around the fall of the Roman Empire (476 CE). However, astrologers frequently faced persecution whenever the practice was seen to be a threat to the authorities. As interest in astrology declined in Europe with the advent of Christianity, in Arab cultures the practice continued and gathered influences from the science and philosophy of the time.

In the fifth century, the Christian Church increasingly came to view astrology as the Devil's work. Nevertheless, many individuals, including high-ranking members of the Church, were sympathetic to astrology throughout the Middle Ages. One prominent example was Pope Leo X, who founded a chair in astrology and astronomy at the papal university.

By the 1700s, astrology's popularity had declined further in England and Europe. This is generally believed to be connected with the advent of the era of Enlightenment, although many scientists at this time – including Copernicus, Brahe, Galileo and Kepler – were themselves astrologers. The astronomical discoveries of these men and others (for example, Copernicus' placing of the Sun at the centre of the universe), shook the foundations of traditional beliefs, including astrology, to their core.

Until this time, astronomy (the scientific study of the stars) and astrology had been practised alongside each other, with no distinction between the two. However, after the Enlightenment, the pursuit of scientific knowledge and the quest for meaning through symbolic methods parted ways and the two subjects became separate entities.

Astrology resurfaced again in Europe in the early nineteenth century and by the turn of the twentieth century had incorporated ideas from the emerging subjects of theosophy and psychology. In particular, the founder of analytical psychology, Carl Jung, drew from occult philosophies, including astrology.

Astrology columns in newspapers and magazines became popular in the 1930s when R. H. Naylor was commissioned to write about the horoscope of the birth of Princess Margaret for the *Sunday Express*. Following the article's overwhelming popularity, he was commissioned to write a weekly prognostication for each Sun sign; thus the horoscope column was born. These columns remain popular to this day and are usually an excellent starting point for developing awareness about the astrological signs. With some further study of the subject one discovers that astrology is a much more rich and complex system than we may first have thought.

Example of a birth chart

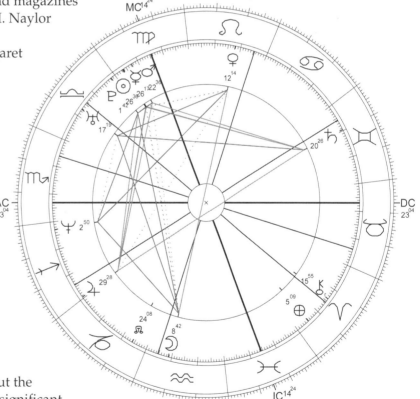

THE HOROSCOPE

A birth chart, natal chart or horoscope provides astronomical information about the position of the planets, signs and other significant

points for a particular moment in time – whether the birth of a person or the start of an event. The chart is drawn up for the time and location of a birth or other significant moment. This horoscope diagram can then be used as a map which contains symbolic information about an individual's character and life experiences.

It can be extremely rewarding, although time-consuming, to draw a birth chart by hand (there are books and astrology courses showing how to do this). Drawing a horoscope by hand takes a great deal of practice and involves the use of tables of astronomical data, including an Ephemerides. For many millennia this was the only way to calculate a birth chart, but these days computer programmes can generate a birth chart in seconds and there are numerous websites offering this service.

To make a birth chart, you will need your birth date, location of where you were born (for example, London) and an accurate time of birth. If the time is not known, the birth chart is often set for noon on the day of birth.

THE PLANETS

The planets represent the different drives within us. Each planet has its own characteristics which, in turn, are coloured by the sign they are placed in at a particular time and in a particular horoscope. The planets operate in the sphere of life represented by the houses in the birth chart.

Although the Sun and Moon are not planets (the Sun is a star and the Moon is a moon), for convenience astrologers often refer to the Sun and Moon as planets or luminaries (celestial bodies which emanate light).

Modern astrologers include the planets from Mercury to Pluto in the birth chart (even though, in 2006, Pluto was reclassified as a 'dwarf planet' by the International Astronomical Union).

As people with different Sun signs will express themselves differently – for example, a person with an Aries Sun could well be confident and assertive, but someone with a Virgo Sun is more likely to be shy and down-to-earth – so those with other planets in their signs may find that the expression of the planets will differ.

For example, the Moon represents qualities of maternity, femininity, the night, mystery, dreams, emotions and moods,

TABLE OF PLANETS

☉	Sun
☽	Moon
☿	Mercury
♀	Venus
♂	Mars
♃	Jupiter
♄	Saturn
♅	Uranus
♆	Neptune
♇	Pluto

TABLE OF ZODIAC SIGNS

Symbol	Zodiac sign	Ruling planet	Element	Mode
♈	Aries	Mars	Fire	Cardinal
♉	Taurus	Venus	Earth	Fixed
♊	Gemini	Mercury	Air	Mutable
♋	Cancer	Moon	Water	Cardinal
♌	Leo	Sun	Fire	Fixed
♍	Virgo	Mercury	Earth	Mutable
♎	Libra	Venus	Air	Cardinal
♏	Scorpio	Pluto (modern) Mars (traditional)	Water	Fixed
♐	Sagittarius	Jupiter	Fire	Mutable
♑	Capricorn	Saturn	Earth	Cardinal
♒	Aquarius	Uranus (modern) Saturn (traditional)	Air	Fixed
♓	Pisces	Neptune (modern) Jupiter (traditional)	Water	Mutable

the home and family unit. When it is placed in Cancer, the Moon feels at home as the planet and sign share many characteristics and the Moon is the traditional ruler of Cancer. Thus the natural qualities of the Moon are strengthened in Cancer. However, when the Moon is in the opposite sign of Capricorn its emotional nature does not express itself so freely because Capricorn is an earthy, practical sign. This means that the Moon will be expressed in a more reserved and restrained way.

INNER, SOCIAL AND OUTER PLANETS

The Sun, Moon and 'inner planets' of Mercury, Venus and Mars form the foundation of our personalities. They are closest to the Sun, so describe the more conscious, personal and subjective parts of ourselves. They move relatively quickly around the zodiac, so their positions at the moment of our birth are unique to that moment – a couple of hours (the Moon), days (the Sun and Mercury) or weeks (Venus and Mars) before or after that moment, and they would be in a significantly different part of the zodiac.

Jupiter and Saturn are slower moving than the inner planets and are often referred to as the 'social planets'. They help us extend our horizons and reach out to others (Jupiter) and work out the boundaries between ourselves and other people (Saturn). They help us to see ourselves in relation to others and to develop a more objective viewpoint.

The 'outer planets' of Uranus, Neptune and Pluto are furthest from the Sun and therefore the slowest moving of all. People born within a certain age range will have these planets in the same area of the zodiac because the planets spend a long time in each sign. Thus they are thought to represent generational trends and describe the collective in which we operate rather than our individual personalities. As they are the furthest planets from the Sun, they represent the unconscious realm.

☉ The Sun

The Sun represents the self and a person's core identity. It gives each individual a sense of purpose and personal goals and is the source of our energy, health and vitality. It rules the heart and plays a central role in integrating the various planets and other components of the birth chart. It describes the talents and natural abilities that need to be developed during the course of a person's lifetime. When you are recognised for your talents and fulfilling your greatest potential, your Sun shines brightly and brings a sense of fulfillment and joy which you can spread to others.

☽ The Moon

The Moon represents our emotional and receptive nature. It describes the type of nurturing we need from our mothers and the kind of nurturing we give to our children and others in our care. It is associated with childhood and our memories of the past. It influences the way in which we relate to others, especially in our home and family life. The Moon is known for its changing phases over the course of the month and signifies our shifting moods as well as our daily life, routines, habits, hobbies and interests.

☿ Mercury

Mercury, the messenger of the gods, represents the intellect and the way in which we express our ideas. It also symbolises our mastery of language and other forms of communication. Mercury is never more than 28° away from the Sun in the birth chart and it acts as the Sun's assistant, helping us to achieve our goals. Mercury is a fast-moving planet which sometimes travels in an apparently backward direction (described as retrograde). This contributes to its reputation as a trickster – Mercury does not always behave as expected and can surprise and fool us; this may lead to misunderstandings and delays.

♀ Venus

Venus, named in honour of the goddess of love, is said to be concerned with our desires, including those of a romantic nature. It can describe the kind of love relationships we are looking for and define who and what we are attracted to. It influences the decisions we make, especially when it comes to deciding what we value. It also refers to self-esteem and the way in which we take care of ourselves and indulge in things that give us pleasure! Venus is often associated with money; its position in the birth chart describes how we bring wealth into our lives.

♂ Mars

Mars, named after the god of war, represents the active principle and is the planet most concerned with the way in which we assert ourselves in the world. It drives us to get what we want and achieve our goals. The planet has a reddish hue because of iron deposits on its surface; this has led to it being associated with violence and bloodshed. Mars rules our primal instincts, anger, passions and sexual conquests. This planet has a strongly competitive streak and loves to win; it is constantly seeking challenges to prove itself to others.

♃ *Jupiter*

Jupiter, the supreme god in the Roman pantheon (also known as Zeus by the Greeks) represents the urge for growth, expansion and wisdom. It is concerned with the beliefs and philosophies that colour our lives. Jupiter values freedom and needs to be able to explore new ideas and experiences. Travel and education are associated with this planet. Through these pursuits we can expand our knowledge and grow as individuals. As the largest planet in the solar system, Jupiter is linked with excess and may represent a tendency to go to extremes and of not knowing when to stop.

♄ *Saturn*

Saturn, the ruler of the Golden Age in Greek and Roman mythology, represents law and order. It is concerned with structures, from the social structures and traditions of society to the skeletal structure of the human body. Saturn also represents boundaries and, as the furthest planet visible to the ancients, marked the edge of the solar system for many millennia. Today it forms the boundary of the 'inner planets'. Beyond Saturn lie the more recently discovered 'outer planets'. Saturn is the inner old man, teacher and authority figure, forcing us to fulfil our responsibilities and work hard to develop our talents and achieve our ambitions in the world.

♅ *Uranus*

Uranus, the sky god, represents the sudden inspiration that comes like a lightning bolt out of the blue, bringing unexpected changes. This planet is associated with original, unconventional ideas and progressive thinking, and is linked with technological invention and social change. Uranus rebels against old ideas and traditions that hold us back as a society and pursues humane ideals such as freedom, equality and justice for all. The planet has come to be associated with science and astrology and the knowledge that these subjects can bring to humanity.

♆ *Neptune*

Neptune, the Roman god of the sea, represents the collective waters of the unconscious through which we are all connected. The source of our imagination and creativity, the planet is concerned with connecting and merging with others and becoming part of the larger whole. It is a planet of compassion and empathy, but it dissolves boundaries. This can make it difficult to distinguish between ourselves and others, creating a fog of confusion and prompting us to use our creative instincts to navigate our path forward.

♇ *Pluto*

Pluto – known as Hades to the Greeks – is the ruler of the underworld in Greek and Roman mythology. The planet represents the ability to delve deeply and uncover long-forgotten secrets and hidden treasures that bring transformation and regeneration. It is linked with the cycle of death and rebirth and can be a brutal force of nature, bringing destruction and change in its wake. Pluto rules the survival instinct and tends to work on an unconscious level, bringing about what we need – often before we know that we need it.

A note on Chiron

The planetoid Chiron has been frequently used in astrology since its discovery in 1977. In mythology, Chiron the Centaur was known as the 'wounded healer' and the planetary body has become associated with wounds and healing in astrology. Its sign and position in the birth chart represent a wounded part of ourselves that serves as a painful reminder of ways in which we feel inadequate and unable to function. Sometimes we will compensate by overdeveloping the qualities of the sign in which Chiron is placed and the planet will sometimes drive us to achieve what we thought was impossible.

Planetary rule

Each planet is said to 'rule' a sign of the zodiac (see Table of Planets on page 174 and Table of Zodiac Signs on page 175). Before the discovery of the outer planets (Uranus in 1781, Neptune in 1846 and Pluto in 1930), only the inner planets had rulership over the signs. However, since their discovery, the three outer planets have been ascribed rulership of three of the signs and are usually considered alongside the traditional rulers.

A planet tends to be most comfortable and its function strongest when placed in the sign that it rules. However, there are no good or bad planetary placements, just different ones which have their own strengths and

A NOTE ON THE TROPICAL AND SIDEREAL ZODIACS

There are two main zodiacs in use – the tropical (mainly used in Western astrology) and sidereal (mainly used in the Vedic astrology of India). The tropical zodiac places 0° Aries at the spring equinox point, around 20 March, as it was in ancient Mesopotamia in the fifth century BCE. However, because of a wobble in the Earth's axis, this has changed over the millennia and the zodiac has shifted backwards by approximately 24° in relation to the time of year.

The sidereal zodiac used in Indian astrology takes this wobble into consideration and adjusts the position of the signs accordingly. Thus, at the present time, 0° Aries in the tropical zodiac is around 6° Pisces in the sidereal zodiac (0° Aries - 24° = 6° Pisces).

For our purposes, we will use the tropical zodiac, which most Western astrologers use today.

weaknesses. The way in which a planet functions will often depend on how we choose to use it. Whichever sign our planets are placed in, they will function in their own unique way in relation to the rest of the birth chart.

THE SIGNS OF THE ZODIAC

Along the outer rim of the birth chart we find the signs of the zodiac, from Aries to Pisces. These signs, which are familiar to most of us, are based on the constellations – groups of stars that have been associated with the characters of myths and epic tales since ancient times. The constellations stretch across an imaginary belt that encircles the Earth – known as the zodiac belt. Conveniently, this belt lies close to the apparent path of the Sun (known as the ecliptic), along with the path of the Moon and planets, and we can follow the journey of each of these celestial bodies in relation to the zodiac sign, or constellation, in which they are placed at a particular moment.

Since the constellations cover different amounts of space and overlap one another along the zodiac belt, it is impossible to have a clear idea about where one ends and the next begins. Therefore, for the purposes of simple and accurate measurement, the division of the constellations was simplified by the Ancient Greeks, who divided the zodiac circle into twelve equal parts of 30° each, one for each of the twelve constellations, or signs, of the zodiac.

The thirteenth constellation in the zodiac belt – Ophiuchus, located between the constellations of Scorpio and Sagittarius – has never been included in the astrological pantheon. This is largely because a circle cannot easily be divided into thirteen parts and the Ancient Greeks wanted to simplify the system so that it was easier to calculate as well as more symbolically functional.

Each of the twelve signs is associated with particular characteristics. Each planet in the birth chart is placed in one of the signs of the zodiac. For example, the Sun represents our essence and core identity. When the Sun is in a particular sign at the moment of birth, our core identity is ascribed with the characteristics of that sign.

While many of us identify strongly with the characteristics of our Sun's sign, some of us do not. This is often because the signs in which the Ascendant, Sun, Moon and other planets are placed in the birth chart combine to make up a person's character. The influence of the other celestial bodies sometimes affects, or overrides, the way we express our

Sun sign. If this is the case for you, it is helpful to find out the sign of your Ascendant, Moon and other planets in your personal birth chart, to see if you identify with them more strongly than you do with your Sun sign.

The signs of the zodiac and the seasons

While 0° Aries marks the vernal equinox and the first day of spring in the northern hemisphere, 0° Cancer marks the summer solstice, 0° Libra marks the autumn equinox and 0° Capricorn marks the winter solstice point (see the section on cardinal signs opposite).

The twelve signs represent the natural cycle of the year. In the northern hemisphere, the first six signs span spring and summer, the sunshine-filled months of birth and growth to maturity when the countryside is clothed in flowers and lush greenery and crops are sown and later harvested. As Virgo gives way to Libra, autumn sets in, the Sun loses its warmth, the fields lie brown and empty and we get ready for the cold, barren winter months. With the return of Pisces, change is in the air, rebirth is around the corner and the wheel has turned full circle.

These seasons are reversed for locations in the southern hemisphere.

THE ELEMENTS

Each of the astrological signs belongs to one of the four elements – fire, earth, air or water. These elements are sometimes referred to as the triplicities because there are three signs in each element.

A predominance of planets in fire and air signs in a birth chart can indicate an extrovert, active nature; a predominance of planets in earth and water signs may indicate an introvert, passive nature (although this also depends on the other factors in the birth chart, such as the position of the planets and sign on the Ascendant).

If you have an emphasis in some elements, the description for those elements will fit your personality much better. If one or two elements are missing in a birth chart, for example, if you have no planets in earth or fire signs, those qualities will tend to be underdeveloped or overdeveloped (because the individual will sometimes compensate for the missing element).

Fire – Aries, Leo and Sagittarius

Fire is associated with energy, activity, vitality, initiation, growth, change, confidence, enthusiasm, faith, curiosity, exploration, play, youth, inspiration, creativity, excitement, impulse, strength, passion, anger, aggression, challenge, competition, generosity and extroversion.

Earth – Taurus, Virgo, Capricorn

Earth represents physical matter, comfort, the senses, sensibility, practicality, stability, security, dependability, groundedness, responsibility, commitment, discipline, skills, talents, tradition, laws, nature, gravity, acceptance and introversion.

Air – Gemini, Libra, Aquarius

Air is the element of the mind, intellect, ideas, discoveries, reason, argument, objectivity, perspective, humanity, ideals, freedom, equality, justice, progress, reform, sharing, exchange, communication, friendliness and extroversion.

Water – Cancer, Scorpio, Pisces

Water represents the emotions, the unconscious, instinct, imagination, dreams, visions, feelings, love, empathy, compassion, sensitivity, needs, depth, mystery, acceptance, forgiveness, adaptability and introversion.

THE MODES

Each of the zodiac signs belongs to one of three modes – cardinal, fixed or mutable. The modes are sometimes referred to as the quadruplicities, because there are four signs in each mode. They combine with the elements and planetary rulers to form the characteristics of each sign.

If you have an emphasis in a particular mode, the description for that mode will fit your personality. If one or two modes are missing in a birth chart, for example, if there are no planets in cardinal signs, those qualities may be underdeveloped or overdeveloped because of a tendency to compensate for the missing modes.

Cardinal – Aries, Cancer, Libra, Capricorn

The Sun's entry into the cardinal signs corresponds with the equinox and solstice points of the calendar, around 20 March (0° Aries), 21 June (0° Cancer), 23 September (0° Libra), and 22 December (0° Capricorn). These points mark the changing of the seasons and represent the entry points into a new phase.

Cardinal signs are active, energetic, outgoing and pioneering. They are

always looking for new possibilities and fresh challenges. People with an emphasis in these signs may be social butterflies who thrive on meeting people and opening doors to new opportunities. While they like to initiate projects, the cardinal mode is not known for its staying power and people belonging to these signs may lose interest quickly before moving on to their next scheme.

Fixed – Taurus, Leo, Scorpio, Aquarius

The fixed signs correspond with the height of spring (Taurus), summer (Leo), autumn (Scorpio) and winter (Aquarius).

Fixed signs are stable and reliable. They have the staying power to continue the work initiated by the cardinal signs and bring it to fruition. However, the fixed signs have a reputation for being stubborn and refusing to change and adapt as the situation requires.

Mutable – Gemini, Virgo, Sagittarius, Pisces

The mutable signs correspond with the waning of the seasons, marking the end of spring (Gemini), the harvesting of summer produce (Virgo), the end of autumn (Sagittarius) and the last remnants of winter (Pisces). They mark a time of decline and adaptation to the new.

Mutable signs are adaptable, but they are not good at initiating projects or sticking to routines. They are good at formulating ideas which may later be taken up by the cardinal signs. They also good at bringing projects to a close and harvesting the rewards.

Compatible signs

When considering compatibility, we look at signs that share sufficient similarities with one another to feel comfortable, but have enough differences to keep things fresh and challenging, so that we can grow through our relationships.

It is useful to remember when looking at compatibility that it is the whole birth charts of two people, rather than simply their Sun signs, which have a bearing on their character and relationships. An experienced astrologer will compare the two people's charts, rather than just their Sun signs, to see how they might get along.

Signs with the same element (fire, earth, air or water) are often said to be compatible. For example, Virgos are thought to be compatible with Capricorns because they are both earth signs. However, each sign in a particular element belongs to a different mode, so there will be enough differences between them to keep things interesting.

Opposites attract, as the saying goes, and the same can be true in astrology. Opposite signs tend to find each other attractive and the differences between them can be very exciting, with plenty of sparks flying! However, opposites sometimes repel and unless both sides are able to make allowances for those elements of the other person's character they don't understand, they can be in constant conflict. But if the two people are able to meet each other halfway, it can be an extremely rewarding combination.

It is important to remember that the guide to compatibility in the next section is only a general guide. Relationships should not be selected on the basis of Sun signs, but on how we feel about the other person! We should remember that any combination can be compatible in real life, and we can use astrology to gain insights into how our relationships work and why they are sometimes unsuccessful.

THE TWELVE SIGN TYPES

 *Aries, the Ram*

ARIES

Sun in Aries: 21 March – 19 April
Ruling planet: Mars
Element: Fire
Mode: Cardinal
Compatible Signs: Leo, Libra, Sagittarius
Part of the Body: Head
Characteristics: Strong, powerful, energetic, active, lively, enthusiastic, optimistic, fun-loving, sociable, confident, assertive, effective, competitive, courageous, youthful, innocent, brave, heroic, inspiring, exciting, adventurous, risk-taking, pioneering, honourable. Can be impatient, aggressive, arrogant, proud, insensitive, headstrong.
Professions: Soldier, police officer, security guard, fire fighter, lifeguard, surgeon, company director, athlete, politician, stuntperson, drummer, builder, blacksmith, ironmonger

TAURUS

♉ *Taurus, the Bull*

Sun in Taurus: 20 April – 20 May
Ruling planet: Venus
Element: Earth
Mode: Fixed
Compatible signs: Virgo, Scorpio, Capricorn
Part of the Body: Neck
Characteristics: Cosy, warm, caring, appreciative, sensible, practical, relaxed, reliable, stable, steadfast, grounded, earthy, constant, secure, determined, comfort-loving, sensual, passionate, fertile, pleasure-seeking, tasteful. Can be stubborn, slow, jealous, possessive and afraid of change.
Professions: Cook, baker, singer, musician, decorator, interior designer, furniture maker, landscape designer, gardener, farmer, builder, sculptor, potter, beautician, masseuse, estate agent, financial adviser, accountant

GEMINI

♊ *Gemini, the Twins*

Sun in Gemini: 21 May – 20 June
Ruling planet: Mercury
Element: Air
Mode: Mutable
Compatible signs: Libra, Sagittarius, Aquarius
Parts of the body: Shoulders and arms
Characteristics: Intelligent, bright, quick-witted, capable, imaginative, talkative, charming, congenial, sociable, curious, energetic, enthusiastic, stimulating, entertaining, playful, fun-loving, adaptable, versatile, youthful, risk-taking. Can be unreliable, inconsistent and dishonest.
Professions: Writer, reporter, columnist, social commentator, presenter, teacher, researcher, matchmaker, wedding planner, salesperson, advertising executive, comedian, entertainer, mimic, magician, counsellor, psychotherapist

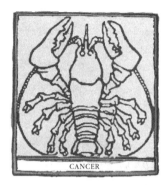

♋ *Cancer, the Crab*

Sun in Cancer: 21 June – 22 July
Ruling planet: Moon
Element: Water
Mode: Cardinal
Compatible signs: Scorpio, Capricorn, Pisces
Parts of the body: Stomach, mammary glands
Characteristics: Sensitive, emotional, instinctive, receptive, good listener, caring, gentle, nurturing, home-loving, private, secretive, enigmatic, imaginative, strong on the outside and soft on the inside. Can be oversensitive, easily offended, moody, defensive, insecure.
Professions: Midwife, nanny, nurse, carer, social worker, primary school teacher, homemaker, landlord/lady, hotelier, caterer, cook, baker, interior decorator, librarian, local historian, collector, museum curator

♌ *Leo, the Lion*

Sun in Leo: 23 July – 22 August
Ruling planet: Sun
Element: Fire
Mode: Fixed
Compatible signs: Aries, Sagittarius, Aquarius
Parts of the body: Heart, spine and back
Characteristics: Confident, creative, lively, joyful, enthusiastic, fun-loving, playful, generous, open-hearted, gregarious, glamorous, loyal, noble, honourable, dignified, likes limelight, feeling special and spreading joy and good fortune with others. Can be egotistical, self-centred, attention-seeking, loud, demanding, bossy.
Professions: Actor, presenter, model, artist, celebrity, clothes designer, company director, PR manager, event planner, fire fighter, lifeguard, politician, dignitary, king/queen!

VIRGO

♍ *Virgo, the Virgin*

Sun in Virgo: 23 August – 22 September
Ruling planet: Mercury
Element: Earth
Mode: Mutable
Compatible signs: Taurus, Capricorn, Pisces
Part of the Body: Intestines
Characteristics: Intelligent, thoughtful, sensible, down-to-earth, conscientious, diligent, discerning, particular, humble, quiet, shy, subtle, witty, hardworking, helpful, useful, reliable, independent, skilled, capable, organised, tidy, clean, hygienic. Can be overly critical, self-deprecating, perfectionist, obsessive, a worrier.
Professions: Teacher, writer, editor, publisher, translator, linguist, critic, librarian, judge, advocate, quality controller, surveyor, administrator, event organiser, craftworker, tailor, tradesperson, restorer, apprentice, nurse, doctor, vet, nutritionist, homeopath

LIBRA

♎ *Libra, the Scales*

Sun in Libra: 23 September – 22 October
Ruling planet: Venus
Element: Air
Mode: Cardinal
Compatible signs: Aries, Gemini, Aquarius
Parts of the body: Kidneys
Characteristics: Charming, sociable, loving, romantic, diplomatic, tactful, attractive, flirtatious, graceful, balanced, harmonious, moderate, peaceful, optimistic, idealistic, objective, clear, logical, just, fair, agreeable, pleasant, relationship-oriented, team player. Can be vain, lazy, dependent, indecisive, argumentative, devil's advocate.
Professions: Architect, mathematician, accountant, salesperson, designer, photographer, make-up artist, beautician, hairdresser, model, ballet dancer, florist, relationship counsellor, mediator, judge, advocate, politician, ambassador, diplomat

SCORPIO

♏ Scorpio, the Scorpion

Sun in Scorpio: 23 October – 21 November
Ruling planet: Pluto
Element: Water
Mode: Fixed
Compatible signs: Taurus, Cancer, Pisces
Parts of the body: Sexual and reproductive organs
Characteristics: Passionate, sexy, strong, powerful, charismatic, magnetic, deep, insightful, quiet, mysterious, sensitive, observant, deep, focused, still, wise, compassionate, determined, self-controlled, devoted, honest, brave, fearless, able to probe deeply. Can be secretive, controlling, manipulative, jealous, possessive, obsessive, extreme.
Professions: Researcher, archaeologist, tax collector, oil tycoon, deep sea diver, miner, refuse and recycling collector, jeweller, surgeon, radiologist, midwife, funeral director, psychotherapist, magician, detective, private investigator, spy, code-cracker, spin doctor

SAGITTARIUS

♐ Sagittarius, the Archer

Sun in Sagittarius: 22 November – 21 December
Ruling planet: Jupiter
Element: Fire
Mode: Mutable
Compatible signs: Aries, Gemini, Leo
Parts of the body: Hips, thighs, liver
Characteristics: Open, honest, optimistic, jolly, fun-loving, energetic, enthusiastic, curious, intrepid, adventurous, pioneering, independent, freedom-loving, youthful, progressive, visionary, imaginative, daring, audacious, expansive, inspiring, philosophical, objective. Can be tactless, careless, restless, bored easily, non-committal, fanatical, risk-taking.
Professions: Student, teacher, academic, researcher, philosopher, journalist, travel writer, explorer, innovator, astronaut, salesperson, bookie, stuntperson, racing driver, athlete, archer, monk, nun, priest, guru

♑ *Capricorn, the Goat*

Sun in Capricorn: 22 December – 19 January
Ruling planet: Saturn
Element: Earth
Mode: Cardinal
Compatible signs: Taurus, Cancer, Virgo
Parts of the body: Skin, teeth and bones
Characteristics: Responsible, stable, sensible, practical, reliable, conscientious, disciplined, determined, capable, successful, smart, professional, ambitious, career-focused, high-powered, hard-working, dedicated, realistic, mature, prudent, careful, reserved, traditional, conservative, self-controlled, punctual. Can be judgemental, pessimistic, callous, authoritarian.
Professions: Banker, accountant, politician, judge, lawyer, police officer, army general, sports coach, head teacher, examiner, civil servant, bureaucrat, manager, director, chiropractor, osteopath, palaeontologist, doctor, dentist, priest

♒ *Aquarius, the Water Bearer*

Sun in Aquarius: 20 January – 18 February
Ruling planet: Uranus (new ruler) and Saturn (traditional ruler)
Element: Air
Mode: Fixed
Compatible signs: Gemini, Libra, Sagittarius
Parts of the body: Ankles, shins, circulation
Characteristics: Independent, lively, friendly, communicative, helpful, humane, socially conscious, idealistic, rebellious, revolutionary, honest, fair-minded, reasonable, even-tempered, cool, clear, intellectual, objective, detached, quirky, eccentric, inventive, innovative, original, cutting edge, visionary. Can be out of touch with emotions, extreme, fanatical, shocking, unrealistic.
Professions: Scientist, astronomer, physicist, meteorologist, mathematician, engineer, inventor, academic, astronaut, politician, activist, reporter, community worker, charity worker, volunteer, electrician

♓ *Pisces, the Fish*

Sun in Pisces: 19 February – 20 March
Ruling planet: Neptune (new ruler) and Jupiter
  (traditional ruler)
Element: Water
Mode: Mutable
Compatible signs: Cancer, Virgo, Scorpio
Parts of the body: Feet
Characteristics: Kind, caring, sensitive, shy,
  emotional, loving, compassionate, soft,
  delicate, passive, impressionable, giving,
  imaginative, dreamy, artistic, spiritual, religious, mysterious, ethereal,
  visionary. Can be oversensitive, insecure, self-sacrificial, impractical,
  unreliable, unrealistic, vague, confused.
Professions: Nurse, carer, anaesthetist, mental health worker, social
  worker, hypnotist, regression therapist, actor, mimic, poet, artist,
  painter, photographer, musician, sailor, swimming instructor, psychic,
  priest, ascetic, mystic, saint

THE AXES

The two axes of the birth chart represent the cross of matter and are its
basic structure.

The Ascendant–Descendant axis runs horizontally across the birth
chart and marks the horizon line for the particular moment and location
of birth. Everything above the horizon indicates that which is in the sky
above, and everything below it shows all that was hidden beneath the
horizon at the moment of birth.

The Ascendant marks that which is rising in the east at the moment of
birth; in astrology it represents the self and a person's appearances. The
Descendant marks that which is setting in the west and represents 'the
other' in the birth chart. This axis is concerned with our personal identity
and our relationships with others.

The Midheaven-Imum Coeli (meaning 'lowest heaven') axis runs
vertically down the birth chart and can be abbreviated to the initials
MC-IC axis. The MC marks the highest point in the sky (the southernmost
point in the northern hemisphere and the northernmost point in
the southern hemisphere), while the IC marks the lowest point (the

CHART OF THE AXES AND HOUSES

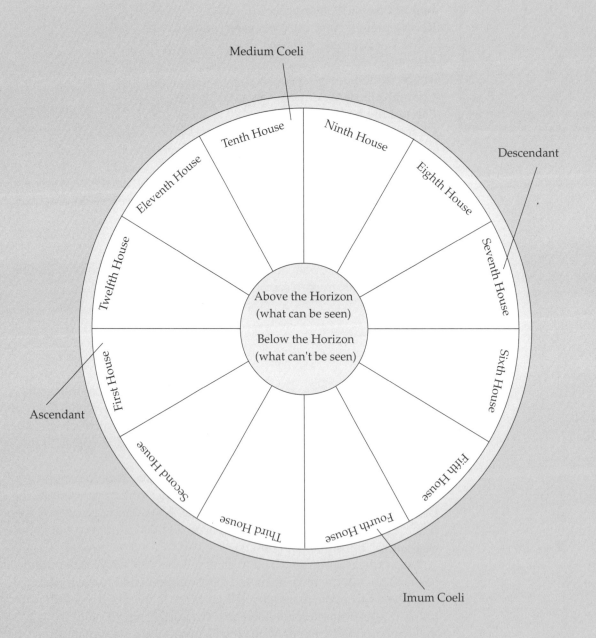

Medium Coeli

Tenth House

Ninth House

Eleventh House

Eighth House

Descendant

Twelfth House

Seventh House

Above the Horizon
(what can be seen)

Below the Horizon
(what can't be seen)

First House

Sixth House

Ascendant

Second House

Fifth House

Third House

Fourth House

Imum Coeli

northernmost point in the northern
hemisphere and the southernmost
point in the southern hemisphere). The
MC represents goals, ambitions and
achievements and the IC represents root,
home and background. It is often called
the parental axis, as the MC is thought to
represent our experience of mother and
the IC our experience of father (although
some people use the opposite meanings
of MC as father and IC as mother – try it
out and see what suits you best).

THE HOUSES

There are twelve houses in an astrological
chart, each one representing a different
sphere of life. The descriptions of each
house correspond to the meaning of the
twelve signs, with the 1st house sharing
qualities with Aries, the 2nd house with
Taurus and so on, to the 12th house
which shares qualities with Pisces.
The houses are marked around the birth
chart circle in an anti-clockwise direction,
starting at the Ascendant.

There are many different house
systems (ways of dividing up time and
space in the birth chart) in use. Two of the
most popular are the Placidus and Equal
House systems.

Once we have identified the signs of
the zodiac in which the planets of our
birth chart are placed, we can look at the
houses in which these planets reside and
find out the sphere of life they affect.
Keywords for each of the houses are
included in the table to the right.

HOUSE	SPHERE OF LIFE
1st	The self, personal identity and appearances
2nd	Security, values, self-worth, finances and assets
3rd	Short-distance travel, communications, siblings and peers
4th	Foundations, home, family background and ancestors
5th	Self-expression, creativity, children, play and risk-taking
6th	Daily life, habits, work and health
7th	Relationships, business partners, adversaries
8th	Shared resources, inheritance, death and intimacy
9th	Long-distance travel, higher education, philosophy and religion
10th	Ambition, goals, social status and profession
11th	Friends, community, groups, social and political ideals
12th	The unconscious, spirituality, institutions and hidden adversaries

EXAMPLE BIRTH CHART – PRINCE WILLIAM

Prince William is the grandson of Queen Elizabeth II and second in line to the throne of the United Kingdom, after his father Charles, the Prince of Wales.

Unlike most of us, William has had a public role to play from the

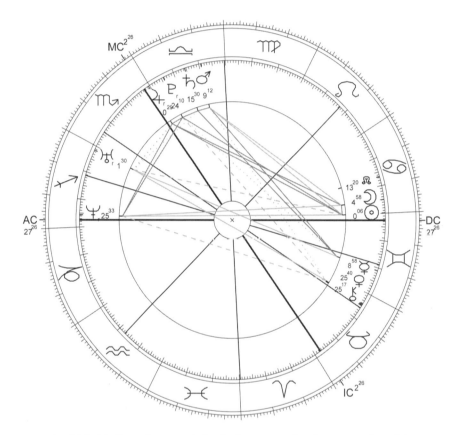

moment of his birth and a great deal of expectation has rested on his shoulders from a young age. While his life is very different from most people's, it is interesting to look at his birth chart and compare it with what we know about his life to see how astrology can be used as a tool for gaining insight into a person's character and experiences.

This section includes a description of each of the planets and signs in William's chart and the houses in which they fall. It is important to synthesise each of these (often conflicting) meanings when reading a birth chart to gain a more accurate impression of the various sides of a person's character. Other factors also come into play, such as the connections between the planets (known as the aspects), but we do not have space to explore them here. We will focus on the aspect known as the conjunction – when two planets are next to each other in the birth chart. With the conjunction, the meanings of the two planets merge and colour each other and add another layer to the way they function in a person's life.

PRINCE WILLIAM'S BIRTHDAY

Prince William was born on 21 June 1982 at 9:03 pm in Paddington, London, England. His birth took place on the longest day of the year in the northern hemisphere – the summer solstice. This day marks the start of the summer season and symbolises the time at which the Sun's power is at its greatest. It represents a time of hope, passion and purpose and the Prince's birth on this day suggests that he embodies these qualities.

The birth of a future monarch is always a time of great celebration and renewed hope, for his family as well as the rest of the nation, as it ensures the continuation of a national institution and its traditions. Celebration of the news of William's birth was no doubt heightened by the significance of the day on which it was announced. We can keep this in mind as we look at the main components of his chart.

Elements and modes

A quick glance at the balance of elements and modes in the birth chart gives an initial idea of the overall balance of the chart and whether any particular qualities are over-emphasised or missing.

We can see that the four elements and three modes are all present in William's chart, with an emphasis on the cardinal water and air signs of Cancer and Libra. The cardinal quality suggests that the Prince is naturally outgoing, friendly and sociable and likes to be proactive and to initiate new ideas and projects. The cardinal signs of Cancer and Libra are both concerned with relating to others and forming relationships and this will therefore be a strong focus for him.

The fire and earth elements are under-represented in the Prince's chart, with the Ascendant and two outer planets in the mutable fire sign of Sagittarius and only Venus and Chiron in the fixed earth sign of Taurus. This suggests that the Prince will rely on his Sagittarian Ascendant for his

motivation, and on his Taurean Venus to keep him stable and grounded.

Sun and Moon in Cancer, in the 7th House

The Sun represents our core identity, sense of purpose and goals and the Moon represents the receptive, emotional, instinctive side of our character.

With William's Sun and Moon close to each other in the sensitive and nurturing sign of Cancer, home and family life are highlighted for the Prince. The Moon rules the sign of Cancer, so it is particularly strong and at home in this sign. The family unit from which he comes, and the tradition that his family represents, are likely to be very important to him.

This double placement of Sun and Moon in Cancer heightens and reinforces his sense of allegiance to his family, his dependency on their support and his feelings of protectiveness towards them.

The Sun also represents our image of father and the Moon our image of mother. With both planets in nurturing and protective Cancer, it is possible that William felt a great deal of care and loving protection from both his parents as he grew up in the public eye.

William's birth not only coincided with the summer solstice, but also with a New Moon and a partial solar eclipse which took place just hours before his birth. A solar eclipse occurs when the Moon passes in front of the Sun as viewed from a position on Earth, obscuring the Sun's light and resulting in a temporary blackout. Eclipses are traditionally seen as omens of fated events and people born at the time of an eclipse often sense that they have a special purpose or task to perform, which will become clear as their life unfolds. What this purpose will entail in William's case remains to be seen and may be related to reforming the traditions he will inherit.

The symbolism of the eclipse may describe his mother's enormous popularity, which often appeared to eclipse his father's position with the public. His parents' separation in 1992 would have been very difficult for William, for whom family life means a great deal. With the Sun and Moon in nurturing and family-oriented Cancer, it is likely that settling down and starting his own family will be extremely satisfying to him.

William has the Sun in Cancer on the Descendant of his birth chart. This is a placement he shares with his mother, along with the Ascendant in Sagittarius. Astrological themes are often repeated in families and they can represent a strong affinity between two family members. This setting position for the Sun is traditionally an auspicious sign for a monarch. It also suggests that William's life will be lived out in the public eye and his interaction with the public, and relationships in general (7th house), will help him build his identity and sense of purpose in the world (the Sun).

Ascendant in Sagittarius

William's Ascendant is in the bright, active sign of Sagittarius. It is also the main source of fire in his chart. The Ascendant represents our appearance and the aspect of our character other people first notice when they meet us. With Sagittarius in this position, William comes across as strong and energetic with a positive outlook on life. Sagittarius in the Ascendant often belongs to people who are youthful, footloose and fancy free. They don't like to take things too seriously and remain good-humoured with a strong sense of perspective, even in times of adversity.

People with this Ascendant placement also like to expand their horizons through travel and exploration of other cultures, philosophies and traditions. William will no doubt enjoy the travel opportunities brought by his royal responsibilities.

The Ascendant in Sagittarius also represents the intrepid explorer. It is clear from his early choice of a career in the armed forces that William is keen to test the limits of his bravery. While his position as second in line to the throne prevents him from active service, William has taken part in undercover operations with the Royal Air Force and the Royal Marines and has served as a search-and-rescue helicopter co-pilot.

Mercury in Gemini, in the 5th House

Mercury is strong in Gemini, as the planet rules this sign. This placement indicates that William's mind is quick and curious and he will have a wide range of interests. Mercury in Gemini needs to share information and network with others. William's wide circle of friends and acquaintances will help satisfy his restless curiosity and he will enjoy meeting people from all walks of life and be genuinely interested in their ideas and experiences.

Mercury in Gemini can also indicate that William's own thoughts are difficult to pin down; commitment to ideas, plans or decisions can sometimes be difficult for this placement. Having the freedom to make his own choices will be important to him, but this may be complicated by the limitations imposed on him by his position. He will probably find a way to work creatively within these limitations and perhaps bend the rules on occasion!

Mercury in Gemini in the 5th house can also indicate a talent for creative writing, drama and wordplay. William possibly has a strong talent

for solving puzzles and riddles. It signifies a good sense of humour and a tendency not to take things too seriously.

Venus and Chiron in Taurus, in the 5th House

Venus is yet another planet in William's birth chart. This planet is placed in the sign it rules, the earthy and luxury-loving Taurus. This placement suggests that William enjoys the good things in life and takes pleasure in home comforts. Since Venus is the only planet (along with Chiron) in an earth sign, it is possible that William will find stability through his relationships. Venus represents constancy and reliability, bringing balance to his watery Sun and Moon in Cancer, which can be moody and temperamental at times. It also brings some grounding to the rest of his chart. Venus in Taurus will not want to rush into relationships, but take its time getting to know the other person, as we have seen with William's seven-year courtship of Kate.

Venus is in the same degree of Taurus as Chiron, the planet which represents wounds and healing. It is a sensitive spot in William's chart; in the 5th house, it suggests that the path of love and romance may not always run smoothly for him.

Mars in Libra, in the 9th House

Mars, the planet of action, passion and adventure is in the gentle, airy sign of Libra in the Prince's birth chart. This suggests that he will have strong ideals and fight passionately for his principles and work tirelessly for what he believes to be right and fair. Mars in Libra is also known for its skills in diplomacy and William will probably have got used to relating to people from all walks of life from an early age. He is good at finding common ground between people and helping to resolve conflicts when they arise.

Mars is next to Saturn in Libra. Saturn encourages William to work hard to achieve his goals. The planet may have an inhibiting effect on Mars and

William's actions and self-assertion will be more careful and measured as a result.

Pluto is also in Libra, although much further away. It is too distant to influence Mars and Saturn (the limit of influence between planets is normally 8°).

Jupiter in Scorpio, on the Midheaven

Jupiter, the planet of growth and expansion, is in the deep, watery sign of Scorpio. Jupiter here likes to be stretched to the limit and may go to extremes in the pursuit of meaningful experiences. Jupiter in Scorpio also suggests that the Prince relishes exploring deep waters. He did so during his military training when he worked on covert underwater operations on submarines. Such adventures would have been greatly satisfying for him.

Jupiter is located at the end of the 9th house and next to the Midheaven in Scorpio in the birth chart. This represents William's goals and direction in life and suggests he will enthusiastically pursue his goals and go to great lengths to achieve whatever he sets out to do. Jupiter also represents kings and royalty; Jupiter on the Midheaven in William's case describes his royal career.

Jupiter is the *chart ruler*, as it rules William's Sagittarian Ascendant. Therefore the planet's position has a greater significance in the birth chart and gives further insight into the way William expresses his Ascendant and interacts with the world. In secretive Scorpio, Jupiter adds a mysterious element to the normally open and straightforward Sagittarian Ascendant; William will need his privacy with this placement. Jupiter in Scorpio also brings an extra dose of charisma and magnetism to William's Sagittarian Ascendant, giving the Prince a natural ability to stand out from a crowd when he wants to and hide from the public eye when he does not.

Jupiter in Scorpio is adept at picking up subtle signals. William will be sensitive to emotional undercurrents and know what other people are feeling. This natural ability to read people will help William in his work and his dealings with others, as he will know who he can trust. It will also give him a good nose for opportunities to help him achieve his goals.

Saturn in Libra, in the 9th House

Saturn, the planet of hard work and fulfilling one's duties, is in the sign of idealistic and romantic Libra. While other factors in the chart indicate that William is a sociable person who gets on well with people from every walk of life, this placement of Saturn in Libra suggests that relationships

and relating may sometimes be a struggle. However, he will be willing to work through difficulties and won't give up easily, preferring to stick them out until they are resolved.

Saturn in the 9th house indicates a practical philosophy of life and a strong work ethic. It also indicates that traditions will be meaningful and greatly valued by the Prince.

The placements of the following three planets apply to the Prince's whole generation, as well as to his own character and experiences.

Uranus in Sagittarius, in the 11th house

Prince William has Uranus in Sagittarius. This represents the desire to learn about and question religious philosophies and traditions and form new ideas based on personal revelations. This generation of individuals is on a quest to discover their own values through thinking and reasoning for themselves. They need the freedom to explore and expand their horizons so that they can see the bigger picture before formulating their own conclusions about life, the universe and everything.

Neptune in Sagittarius, on the Ascendant

Neptune in Sagittarius is thought to represent a generation of idealists with an interest in religious experience, mysticism and religious philosophies from around the world.

Neptune in Sagittarius is close to the Ascendant in Prince William's birth chart and opposite his Sun and Moon at the Descendant. This is quite a prominent placement for this outer planet and it indicates a strong sensitivity to the people and events around him and an ability to empathise with others. William has a natural affinity with the hopes, dreams and yearnings of the collective and will no doubt feel a strong connection with the people he represents.

Neptune on the Ascendant brings a dreamy quality to a person's appearance and indicates someone who can appear very easygoing and malleable on the surface – although this may not be the case on a deeper level. William will find that others can easily project their ideals and high expectations onto him.

Pluto in Libra, in the 9th House

Prince William's Pluto is located in the sign of Libra, in the 9th house. The generation of people born with Pluto in Libra are concerned with finding a new way of relating to others. The young people from this generation have seen many of the marriages of their parents' generation fall apart; they are determined to rewrite the rulebook on romantic relationships, as the traditional relationship structures no longer seem to be reliable. Times have changed and the strict rules about who William's ancestors (up to his father's generation) would have been allowed to marry no longer apply to the Prince.

We have yet to see how Prince William's special destiny will unfold. However, as with the rest of us, his birth chart may offer insights along his life's journey.

DOWSING

Dowsing, also known as 'divining', is a simple but effective practice that anyone can try. With the body or hands as a receptor, this method involves the use of dowsing rods and, sometimes, pendulums to obtain a more amplified reading. These tools have been in use for thousands of years and remain popular today.

Dowsing is an effective way to detect unseen objects, such as underground deposits of water, metals, gems, petroleum and to find archaeological sites and tunnels. It can be used to locate missing persons or mislaid objects and – like most forms of divination – to answer questions.

Dowsing may also be used to detect ley lines – pathways in the landscape along which geographical features and sacred sites have been aligned. There is evidence that ley lines have been used since Neolithic times, possibly to assist with navigating the way across the land before roads and signs were introduced. Ley lines are thought to be areas where energy converges in the landscape and dowsing can pick up on their subtle signals and locate the course of these ancient paths.

Dowsing is often used to tap into energy fields involved in feng shui. It can indicate spots in the home or workplace where our energy may be increased or decreased and where we should encourage – or avoid – long periods of sitting, working and sleeping.

HOW DOES DOWSING WORK?

Exactly how dowsing works remains a mystery. It is a form of *radiesthesia*, which means 'perception of radiation'. This term was coined by the French priest Alex Bouly in the early part of the twentieth century. Although it does not refer to any sort of radiation recognised by science, *radiesthesia* suggests that the technique picks up on a mysterious energy field, like radiation, that is emitted by people, animals and objects in the landscape.

Dowsing does not need to take place on location, however. It can function just as well at a distance, with the dowser using a map or similar tool for guidance. Dowsing can also be used to answer questions, so it is responsive to the mind and the human will.

As with all forms of divination, there is no scientific proof that the use of dowsing to locate underground objects actually works – it may just be a matter of chance. However, practitioners know what an incredibly useful tool it can be in sensing the unseen world around us and in helping to find the objects and answers we need in a simple and effective way.

DOWSING INSTRUMENTS

Dowsing rods usually take the form of a forked branch, known as a *V rod*, *Y rod*, or *witching rod*. They are traditionally made with wood from the witch hazel tree. Dowsing rods may also take the shape of two pieces of wire bent in L-shapes, known as *angle rods*. The dowser holds these loosely in both hands and observes their reaction while walking around a location.

Pendulums can also be used for dowsing. While rods are normally used to divine objects in larger settings, pendulums are useful in smaller locations, for example, for medical use on the body or in the use of maps or images of the location in question, or to answer general questions from a seated position.

A pendulum usually consists of a chain or thread which is weighted with an object – commonly a pointed crystal, ring, pendant or other small, lightweight item.

Other instruments, such as a wand (a straight stick) may also be used, but these are less common. As with all forms of divination, you should use the instrument that feels right for you.

Below: Liberal philosopher John Locke (1632–1704) referred to the ability to divine, or discover, mines of gold and silver.

ORIGINS OF DOWSING

It is not known when or where dowsing originated, but there is evidence that the practice has been used since ancient times. Images of dowsing instruments have been discovered in ancient mosaics from the Middle East and reliefs from China.

Around the fifteenth century, dowsing became a popular means of detecting underground deposits of metals in Germany and the surrounding regions. The practice then spread to England and was used in the mining of metal and coal.

In 1518, Martin Luther, the German priest who initiated the Protestant Reformation, listed dowsing as one of the many occult practices that were outlawed by God.

The philosopher John Locke first used the term 'deusing rod' (later spelled 'dowsing') in a text published in 1692, when he wrote about its use in discovering metals for mining.

Dowsing remained in popular use until the Enlightenment of the eighteenth century, when divinatory practices began to be regarded as superstitious nonsense by the intellectual classes of the time. However, it started to become popular again in the Victorian era, with the growth in interest in occult practices.

The French priests Alex Bouly, Alexis Mermet and Father Jean Jurion are credited with pioneering the use of pendulums for medical use in the early part of the twentieth century. In their method, a pendulum, or simply the hands of the practitioner, could be hovered over the body and any reactions detected were used to diagnose physical ailments. Bouly is also credited with coining the term *radiesthesia* to describe the practice and this word has become particularly associated with the use of pendulums for medical diagnoses.

During the twentieth century, numerous organisations and courses in dowsing were created around the world and dowsers were frequently employed by mining and oil companies and consulted on archaeological digs. Today their skills and advice are often sought by people who are house-hunting and by those who are searching for answers to questions that are difficult to find by other means.

FIRST STEPS IN DOWSING

Anyone can dowse and, with practice, we can all develop dowsing skills. Some people pick it up as soon as the instruments are placed in their hands, but others will need some training in holding the tools and interpreting their movements. There are numerous courses and organisations that offer training in the subject.

You can start to practise dowsing with rods or pendulums as follows:

Step 1: Relax It is important to relax your mind and body, take some deep breaths and sit or stand still for a moment to get in tune with your surroundings.

Step 2: Formulate your question Whatever you would like to find out through dowsing, you will need to formulate the question or visualise the object clearly in your mind. Whether you are searching for water, tunnels, metal or other underground deposits, or just have a question to ask, you will need to focus your mind on it while holding the instrument.

Step 3: Practise Whether dowsing with rods or pendulums, it is useful to start by asking a question you know the answer to and seeing how the instrument reacts. A short practice period each time you use the instrument will help you get in tune with it.

- To practise dowsing with a Y-shaped rod, hold the top forks of the Y-shape in both hands so that they are firmly balanced but loose enough to move of their own accord. Next, ask the dowsing rod to point in the direction of certain objects around you and see how it responds. You may want to distribute a few objects in advance to use as markers for this test. Then you can ask 'Where is the book?', 'Where is the pen?', and so on. Then walk to the object and stand over it to see how the rod responds.

  As you move around, the rod will incline upwards, downwards or twitch a little to indicate that it has detected the item you are searching for. If you ask about the location of an object, the rod may pull or point in a particular direction.

- When using L-shapes rods, hold the short ends of the L-shape in your hands and balance the long ends over the top of your hands so that you are holding them parallel to the ground at all times. Hold them firmly – they should not be allowed to swing around, but neither should they be gripped so tightly that they cannot move freely.

  When the object is directly beneath you, the rods will usually cross in the middle, but use your judgement to see how they respond for you.

- To practise using a pendulum, hold the string or chain between your thumb and forefinger, about two or three inches from the weight at the end and allow the weight to hang down. You might find it useful to have a point at the end of the weight to help show the direction in which it is inclining.

  You can ask the pendulum a question such as 'Where is the book?' and see how it responds. Then hover the pendulum directly over the book and observe its reaction. It may swing from side to side, or spin in a clockwise or anti-clockwise direction when it is above the object.

Once you start to become proficient at dowsing, you may want to test your technique by asking a friend to hide an object somewhere in a room. Then walk around the room while asking the rod or pendulum where the object might be and following its responses until you find what you are looking for. Once you get to know your instrument and its reactions, you will be ready to start dowsing!

ANSWERING QUESTIONS WITH PENDULUMS

Pendulums are often used to answer questions; these questions may be posed either by you or by another person (the querent).

First, make sure you are relaxed. Now suspend the pendulum from your fingers, trying to hold your hand as still as possible. Now you are ready to ask the pendulum a question. Formulate the question in your mind or ask the querent to formulate his or her question carefully and tell you what it is. Then decide which of the following methods would be most useful to you.

Yes or no question

To practice, start by asking a question for which you know the answer is 'yes', and observe how the pendulum responds. Try this a few times. Then ask a question for which you know the answer is 'no'. Repeat this a few times with different questions and observe the instrument's reaction.

When the pendulum swings back and forth in a horizontal line, this is often taken to mean 'no'. When the pendulum swings back and forth in a vertical line, this is taken to indicate 'yes'. When the pendulum swings in a circle, this is sometimes taken to mean 'perhaps'. However, one can also take the clockwise circle to indicate 'yes', and the anti-clockwise circle to indicate 'no'. Decide which system works best for you. Once you have established what each movement indicates, you are ready to ask your question!

General question

The pendulum can be held over words written on a piece of paper or other surface. It will nudge towards the word it wants to use or may start to swing or spin when hovered over the word that answers the question. The more energetically it swings or spins, the more definite the answer.

You need to prepare lists of words or names that are relevant to the question and then see how the pendulum responds to each of them.

To discover the sex of a baby

Using a pendulum to find out the sex of an unborn child is a popular tradition throughout Europe. A wedding ring tied to the end of a thread is often used, but any form of pendulum will work. The pendulum is held over the tummy area or hand of the pregnant woman. If the pendulum starts to spin in a circular motion, this indicates that the baby is a girl. If it swings from side to side, it indicates a boy.

A pendulum can also be held over the hand of a woman who is not pregnant, to indicate the sex of any potential children she may have – the first

response represents the first child, the second response represents the second child and so on until the pendulum stops swinging.

To pinpoint a location on a map

For questions about location or to dowse for underground objects, formulate the question in your mind, then slowly hover the pendulum over the surface of the map to find the answer. When the pendulum hovers over the correct location, it will react by spinning or swinging from side to side.

To find a missing object

Pendulums can be used to locate missing objects. First of all you may want to hold the pendulum over a picture of the object to see how it reacts.

If you know that the object is located somewhere in the room you are in, or nearby, ask the pendulum where the object can be found. If it starts to nudge in a particular direction, follow the direction and hover the pendulum over objects you come across until the pendulum starts to spin – the wider the spin, the closer you are to the object in question. A map can be used if the object is further away.

You can also use yes or no questions to pinpoint the location of the missing object, for example, by asking 'Is X in London?', or 'Is X in a northerly direction from here?' Once the location has been pinpointed, you can go there or use a relevant map, as above.

To find the date of an event

To discover the date or time of an event, formulate your question and then find a calendar for the day, week, month or year to which the question relates. Hover the pendulum over the range of likely days or hours in which an event is likely to occur. The pendulum will start to swing when it finds the answer to the question. The more definite the answer, the wider the swing will be.